Religious Truth for Our Time

William Montgomery Watt, Professor Emeritus of Arabic and Islamic Studies at the University of Edinburgh, is well known as an authority on the life of Muhammad and the origins of Islam. His many books in that field are widely respected and include *Companion to the Qur'ān*, also published by Oneworld.

By the same author

Companion to the Qurʾan
The Faith and Practice of al-Ghazāli
Islamic Fundamentalism and Modernity
The Influence of Islam upon Medieval Europe
Islamic Political Thought
Islamic Philosophy and Theology
Muhammad at Mecca
Muhammad at Medina
Muhammad: Prophet and Statesman
Muhammad's Mecca: History in the Qurʾan
A Short History of Islam
What Is Islam?

RELIGIOUS TRUTH FOR OUR TIME

William Montgomery Watt

ONEWORLD

OXFORD

Religious Truth for Our Time

Oneworld Publications
(Sales and Editorial)
185 Banbury Road
Oxford OX2 7AR
England

Oneworld Publications
(US Marketing Office)
PO Box 830, 21 Broadway
Rockport, MA 01966
USA

ISBN 1-85168-102-7

Printed and bound by
WSOY, Finland

CONTENTS

Preface

This book is for the ordinary thoughtful person and not for the specialist in theology. The author is a Christian who has spent fifty years in the study of Islam, and this has led to the use of more illustrations from Islam than from other religions. The underlying view on which the book is based is that there is much truth in all the great religions, and that this is proved by their fruits – the quality of life seen in their adherents.

How truth is expressed in the religions is affected by the inadequacies in human language and thought, and these are studied in the first two chapters, which show the difficulty, sometimes impossibility, of making an intellectual comparison of the assertions of the different religions. What is important in each religion is its total view of the realities with which human life has to deal from day to day.

Further, the truth in the various religions is seen as coming to them from God. This assertion, however, has to be understood in a way that allows for development in religion. In connection with the Old Testament it will be insisted that the commands God gives to a people are appropriate to the stage of civilization they have reached, and are not necessarily for all time. The same principle will apply to the other religions. Since the religions originated in different social cultures, allowance must be made for the possibility that each has a task assigned to it in God's purposes, though this differs from the task assigned to the Jews and Christians.

My thanks for helpful comments to Fergus Kerr O.P., Novin Doostdar of Oneworld Publications and Martin Forward, but I alone am responsible for the views expressed.

CHAPTER 1

The Inadequacies of Human Thought and Language

Any attempt to justify belief in religious truth must first look at the difficulties faced by the human mind in understanding the world in which it lives and in presenting its religious beliefs in language. These difficulties will be looked at briefly in this first chapter.

The Limitations of Human Language

A distinction is often made between the primary and secondary uses of language, the secondary uses also being described as metaphorical, symbolic or analogical. Sometimes there is a suggestion that what is merely metaphorical is unreal. The language used to express religious truth is largely of a secondary character, and so it becomes important to show that, despite the use of language in this way, religious statements are dealing with reality.

The primary uses of language are to be seen in basic root-words and these doubtless reflect the fundamental experiences of primitive humanity. Nouns represent common objects: tree, dog, leg, shoe, mother, son, sky. Verbs represent actions: run, eat, sit, buy, marry. Adjectives show qualities of objects: sweet, loud, bright, hard. Prepositions show relationships: of, on, through; and adverbs can show relationships and also qualities of actions: down, fast. Some of these simple words have a degree of complexity, which can be described as a pattern. A shoe and a chair are not just objects of a particular shape: a shoe is for wearing on the foot, and a chair is for sitting on.

When we want to speak about something for which there is no primary word we may use a primary word in a secondary sense, as when we say a chair has legs, these legs being something like human or animal legs, or we may combine two primary words: put on, come down. In Latin and Greek, instead of combining two words, prefixes were added to primary words, as in the anglicized forms concur (running together) or sympathy (suffering with). In English we speak of a river running, because this is 'something like' a person or an animal running. We also use the Latin word *current*, and further apply this (in a tertiary sense?) to an electric current. The use of words from Latin and Greek tends to make us unaware that they are secondary uses of simple words.

Language may also be applied in a secondary way to things not perceived by the senses. Scientists talk about atoms, but this is only the Greek word for 'uncut' or 'uncuttable'. Light is said to consist sometimes of waves, sometimes of particles, but this amounts to saying that in certain respects light is something like waves (of the sea) and in other respects something like particles (small material objects). Such secondary uses of language are particularly common in religion, though often masked in English by the use of Latin and Greek derivatives. Thus *transcendent* is merely something which climbs across or beyond the ordinary, and *immanent* is something which flows in other things. From these considerations two important points emerge in respect of religious truth.

First, these secondary uses of words do not give us precise ideas. They only show us that what they denote is something like what is meant by the primary sense of the word. Just as the leg of a chair is only something like a human or animal leg, so God is only something like a father. I have elsewhere suggested that this use of language might be called 'iconic',[1] an icon being a two-dimensional representation of a three- dimensional object, that is, something known to be inadequate, yet accepted as a representation of a reality. Some Islamic theologians held that such terms were to be accepted 'without asking how', that is, without asking whether they were to be understood literally, metaphorically or in some other way; and which might be expressed by the English word *amodally*. This was possibly to oppose a popular view that what was not understood literally was unreal. Because some such view is also found today, the description of language as iconic or amodal refutes the suggestion that what is referred to (in non-literal language) is unreal: there is nothing unreal about waves of light. Similarly in religion, though the terms used are iconic, what they refer to is something real. There may be exceptions, but if so, the unreality of what is referred to has to be determined by criteria other than the iconic character of the language.

Second, when language is used in this secondary way, what would be a contradiction with primary language is not necessarily so. God's being something like a father does not prevent his also being something like a mother; and his being something like beyond the world and humanity (transcendent) does not prevent his being also something like flowing in them (immanent). This possible absence of contradiction is particularly important when comparing different religions. It means that a statement of belief in one religion, apparently contrary to a statement in another, is not necessarily so: the two statements may be compatible when each is understood in its own context. It follows that it is very difficult to compare religions in respect of their formal statements of belief, and may sometimes be impossible. This point might be illustrated from Christianity and Buddhism, since many strands of Buddhist thought seem to deny the existence of God. Thomas Merton, whom I regard as one of the profoundest Christian thinkers of this century, found when talking with Buddhist monks about matters of spirituality that they were very much on the same wavelength.

More important than intellectual comparison is the assessment of religions by their fruits – that is, by the quality of life seen in their adherents individually and as a community. The principle of assessing a religious proclamation by its fruits is found in the New Testament (Matthew 7:15–20). Jesus pointed out that one does not get grapes from thorns or figs from thistles; good fruit comes only from a sound tree, and he was speaking about false prophets or religious leaders. A modern objection might be that it is possible for a theory to 'work' in practice although the theory is not true; but if this happens, it could only be in the case of a single isolated theory, whereas the religions give a comprehensive view of the world in which human beings live.

When the criterion of fruits is applied, it may be claimed that all the great religions have shown good fruits in the lives of their adherents. They have enabled millions of people to live lives that, at least up to a point, were satisfactory and meaningful. There can, of course, be disputes about what precisely constitutes good fruits, but there is probably a wide measure of agreement on this matter and I do not propose to discuss it further.

In conclusion I note that, because of the limitations of language and of the way in which all religions use it, the picture of the world given by the religions is not as complete as a scientist might wish. What is to be emphasized, however, is that the religions give human beings adequate knowledge of the world in which they live and of the higher powers to which they are subject, and that this knowledge is sufficient to form the basis of a satisfactory and meaningful life. There are, of course, other points that could be discussed. It is conceivable that people might base their lives on their religion and yet not find satisfaction; but this would presumably depend on personal matters. It could also be asked what makes individual and social life satisfactory and meaningful, and perhaps it should be allowed that sometimes satisfaction is not realized in this life but only in the light of eternity.

The Social Character of World-Views

All human beings have various deep drives. The most important are to stay alive by getting food, shelter, etc.; to continue the race; and to seek to make life meaningful or significant. There is also a strong tendency to live in communities, but this is perhaps not so much a separate drive as something required to fulfil the other drives. In general, human communities have a continuing life. Sometimes they fade away or are destroyed, and sometimes they are absorbed by other communities; but human beings cannot exist without a community of some kind. There is also an overall tendency for communities to grow larger.

In each community or society a world-view develops, and by this I mean a picture or conception of the world, and especially of the realities with which people have to deal in their lives. This will include a basic cosmology, together with a belief about the nature of the forces controlling human life and the values which people should try to attain in their lives. The pre-Islamic Arabs had a deep-seated belief that most of the events in a person's life, and especially the date of his or her death, were determined by an impersonal force they called Time or Fate. In early societies the world-view and the religion were more or less identical, and had been worked out gradually as a basis for living. People with specially deep religious awareness would make important contributions and so develop the religious aspect. The process of forming a world-view has been called 'the social construction of reality' by Peter L. Berger and Thomas Luckmann in a book of that title.[2] There is also a close connection between world-view and language: the Arabic word for the Time or Fate determining the date of one's death is difficult to translate into languages associated with world-views without this concept of predetermination.

In most early religious world-views the highest place has been given to one or more gods, and the word *god* seems to be a primary word in many languages, meaning an entity or being with some degree of control over human life. There is also the suggestion that this is a form of being that transcends human life, and it may be spoken of as the sacred, the holy or the numinous. It would appear that some human beings, perhaps many or most, have direct experience of the sacred.

In contrast to most world-views of past times, that of Western Europe has changed considerably in recent centuries. This has been due at many points to the advances of science, an obvious example being the abandonment of the belief that the earth is flat. Scientific advances also led to the European Enlightenment of the eighteenth and nineteenth centuries. This was in part an anti-religious movement, for its proponents regarded most religion, and indeed most traditional metaphysics, as superstition. They believed in the omnicompetence of reason and saw it as the agent bringing about progress towards a better state of human society – something they fully expected to come about. Apart from explicit denial of some Christian doctrines by sections of the Enlightenment, the disciplines of historical and literary criticism also developed, and these brought about extensive revision of Christian ideas about the Bible and historical matters. This may also be said to have led to a partial separation of the religious and non-religious aspects of the world-view. Most Westerners accept the non-religious aspects, but retain most of their religious beliefs in so far as they are believers in Christianity or one of the other religions. There are also, of course, humanists, agnostics and atheists. Thus the complete Western world-view is far from being monolithic. Its non- religious aspects, however, are now being more deeply implanted in the Western mind by the power of the media, and also to a great extent in the mind of the rest of the world.

In these non-religious aspects are also to be included many of the values of human life. One of the ideas of the Enlightenment was the autonomy of the moral consciousness, and because of this Christians also came to see conscience as the source of moral truth. Yet it should be clear that conscience itself is largely formed by the world-view of the community and may sometimes be in error. In the nineteenth century, for example, it was widely held by British Christians of most denominations that it was incestuous for a man whose wife had died to marry her sister. This was because 'wife's sister' appeared among the 'forbidden degrees' in the 1662 Church of England Book of Common

Prayer. This, however, was based on a misunderstanding of a rule in the book of Leviticus (18:18), which in a polygamous society forbade the marrying of two sisters at the same time. Marriage to a deceased wife's sister was made legal by Parliament about the middle of the nineteenth century, but was only gradually accepted by many Christians.

Since the early nineteenth century Christians have been trying to come to terms with this new non-religious world-view which has developed in the West. Some have managed to go a long way in the process of reconciliation. Others have tended to retreat into the past and keep the nonreligious world-view and their religion in separate compartments, as it were. Perhaps the chief point to emphasize after the discussions here is that the individual's world-view is usually restricted to that of his or her society with its imperfections. Yet, despite these imperfections, the believer should usually be able to lead a tolerable and meaningful life.

CHAPTER 2

Truth and Factuality

Before considering particular questions about truth in the religions it is important to look at the general nature of truth, especially its relationship to facts.

The Place of Patterns in Human Perception

In the earlier part of this century philosophers spoke much about sense-data, that is, the individual elements of experience given to us by the senses. The term encouraged the assumption that, for example, when one looked at a landscape, one saw a vast number of little blobs of colour which one fitted together to form objects. More recently it has been realized that in actual human perception the order is different. First of all one sees the general features of the landscape, or some of them, and then one may look at some part of it in greater detail. It is only by a process of conscious analysis that one reaches the individual elements. I once tried an experiment with a friend: we were out walking, and I told him to look closely at the shape of a hill on the other side of a stretch of water. After a minute I asked him if he had seen the sheep, and he had to answer 'no'. Yet there were sheep appearing as tiny white dots scattered over the hill, and once his attention was called to them he could not help seeing them.

In my account of how people perceive things I use the

word *pattern*, and I use it in a very wide sense to indicate something complex as distinct from single items such as sense-data. The German word *Gestalt* has been used somewhat similarly. When people look about them, what they see is an all-embracing pattern within which there may be more detailed patterns. If you look at a room, you may have a general impression of the room and the furniture, but then you may focus on one piece of furniture and notice its shape more exactly. It is also possible, of course, to begin by focusing on a particular object within the total field of vision. The importance of patterns in our experience of the world is shown by the fact that some of our primary words have a degree of complexity which may be described as a pattern rather than as a simple object. As was noted above, a chair is not just an object of a certain shape, but one designed for sitting on. Mother, father, son, sister, cousin, denote complex physical and social relationships. So does a verb like *buy*. Some of these examples show that patterns exist not merely in a static field of vision but also in a series of events.

In any manifold there are many different patterns. Some of these may even conflict with one another, especially in historical sequences. Moreover, not all patterns are immediately obvious. Much of the work of scientists consists in looking for patterns that are important for our understanding of natural happenings. Newton's discovery of the law of gravitation was largely due to his noticing a similar pattern in the fall of an apple and in the movement of the planets round the sun. He did not, of course, merely call attention to the pattern, but showed by complex mathematical calculations how it applied to the various phenomena. Moreover, it applied to all the relevant phenomena; there were no exceptions.

With the theory of gravitation we may contrast the phlogiston theory, generally accepted by scientists in the first half of the eighteenth century to account for the phenomena associated with the burning of various materials. The theory was that in many material objects there was a weightless substance called phlogiston, and burning released this substance. If a thing burned easily and quickly, it had much phlogiston; if it burned slowly, it had little; and if it did not burn at all, it had none. Phlogiston may thus be described as a pattern observed in the burning of various materials. As scientists discovered more about gases, however, they found many cases where the supposed phlogiston pattern did not fit the phenomena, and eventually the theory was abandoned. This shows that patterns may really exist in events, and yet not be relevant to their causal explanation. It is the causal explanation in which scientists are primarily interested.

Science may thus be described as the quest for causally important or significant patterns. The items which constitute these patterns may be called facts. For the scientist it is important that all the items comprised in a pattern should be factual, and that no relevant facts should be left out of account. Since at some points there are alternative theories – alternative patterns – the layperson has to rely on the theories and patterns on which all scientists agree, such as the theory of biological evolution; all scientists are agreed that biological evolution has occurred, though they are not agreed about the factors which produced it.

In history the case is somewhat different. Consider historians writing an account of the Thatcher years in British government. Before they complete their work, if not when they begin, they will have an overall view of the period. One will see it as a wonderful success, another as a great calamity, and others as something in between. This is the main pattern, and each historian supports his or her view by the presentation of facts. They have, however, a vast number of facts from which to choose, and these facts are probably much more diverse than those of the scientist. The historian has to decide which facts to regard as important and to include, and which to regard as irrelevant or unimportant and neglect. On these matters historians will decide differently; but in history the criteria for deciding what is relevant and important and what is not are far less clear than in science. Each historian's decisions will depend partly on what may be called his or her values. Because there is wide divergence in values among historians, there is no likelihood in the immediate future of agreement about the general pattern of the Thatcher years. Perhaps a century hence, in the light of what has happened in the interval, historians may be closer to agreement.

Because this is how historians work, we have the paradoxical feature that it is possible to have a false general pattern although the items which constitute it are all genuine facts; and in the course of time there can be wide agreement that some general patterns are false. If one considers the question whether the French Revolution was a good thing or a bad thing, we find shortly after the events that some people vigorously maintained that it was good, while others maintained that it was bad; and both groups could support their views by a selection of true facts. After two centuries, however, it would probably be agreed that it had both good and bad points so that the two extreme views are unbalanced even if not exactly false. In other words, to have a historical account entirely based on true facts does not ensure that it is true. This applies primarily, of course, to overall general views or patterns, not to questions of detail where the values of the individual historian have less play.

From this we move to the question of whether a general pattern can be true, if some of the items composing it are not factual. This question is raised by the findings of literary critics of the Old Testament. They showed that in many cases the books had been edited and re-edited to suit succeeding generations. What we now have is the later editors' views of earlier events and not those of the participants. My answer to the question would be that the general pattern may be true, even when the details constituting it are not all entirely factual.

The point just made may be supported by considering paintings: a picture by a great artist, whether of a person, a bowl of flowers or a landscape, will not usually be identical with a photograph of the same subject. Artists make subtle changes in detail to emphasize what they see as the deeper significance of the whole, and in this respect the painting has not the factuality of the photograph. The artist, however, has portrayed something real which the photograph was incapable of showing. In such cases we could speak of the pictorial truth of a total pattern even though some of the details were not factual. This point was forcibly made by Peter Cornwell;[3] he described a portrait of Lord Hailsham, in All Souls College, Oxford, where the head is surrounded by a mist. The mist was obviously not part of the actual scene before the painter, but it made an important contribution to his presentation of Lord Hailsham, and brought out something of his character and personality that a photograph would not have done. There is something in a person more real and more important than the mere facts recorded by a camera, and thus non-factual elements can play a genuine part in the presentation of an aspect of reality, that is, of a pattern which is a true pattern.

In previous treatments of the subject I have also called attention to the nature of a diagram.[4] The example I used was the plan of the London Underground, where there are a number of vertical and horizontal straight lines and some diagonals. Travellers from A to B are shown with absolute accuracy where they would have to change stations and what stations they would pass. If one asked for more from the diagram, however, it would be misleading. It does not show the exact distance from station to station nor the precise direction of the lines, still less their windings and turnings. Yet despite these shortcomings and inaccuracies, it is a wholly true presentation of the essential information required by travellers. Much the same is true of maps; they are true presentations of a limited range of facts, but beyond that range they can be misleading.

The word *myth* has sometimes been used for what might be called pictorial presentations of reality. Unfortunately the word has also a negative sense, according to which myth is contrasted with reality, and so is necessarily false. Thomas Merton raises some of the questions about the use of this word when he speaks of the American myth, which he formulates in the sentence 'America is the earthly paradise'.[5] He then points out that this was a valid and creative myth, for it comprised the 'belief in the obvious possibilities of an immense new continent'.[6] For four centuries it directed people towards the realization of some of these possibilities. So long as there was a frontier the myth had some validity. Merton holds, however, that in the end the myth turned into a daydream or an evasion that could lead people astray.

Nevertheless he thinks that in general people require myths to live by. The word *myth* is best avoided in such contexts, but we could say that people require a world-view which includes the presentation, perhaps in pictorial form, of the significance and meaning of human life, and of the values it is capable of realizing.

A part of the world-view of the writers of the Bible is that God is able to interfere with natural processes. This is something modern believers cannot accept, since it contradicts the conception of natural law which has an important place in the Western intellectual outlook or world-view.

While the assured results of science should certainly be accepted by believers, they should also realize that the scientific account of the world is far from complete. There may still be natural laws which science has not discovered, and there may be areas of reality not accessible to present scientific methods. Faith-healing undoubtedly occurs, but the scientific explanation is not clear. It is thus possible that some of the events which the Biblical writers ascribe to divine interference with natural processes actually occurred, and are to be explained by a natural law not yet known to science. In many cases, however, some other explanation will be possible of the alleged divine interference; but there are also cases where it is pointless to speculate about what actually happened, such as the ascent of Elijah into heaven (2 Kings 2:9–13). In general the believer will hold that God works through natural processes and not by interfering with them, but that he also influences the conduct of individual human beings by guiding and strengthening them.

An example of an alleged interference where another explanation is obvious is the statement that God caused the sun to stand still in the sky for about a whole day, so that Joshua could inflict an overwhelming defeat on his enemies (Joshua 10:12–14). To a modern believer this would have to mean that the rotation of the earth had been stopped or slowed down, and that is really unthinkable. Presumably what happened was that the victory was so complete and so far beyond expectations that Joshua and his men felt that the day had been made longer for them; but this was essentially a subjective feeling. Then in the telling of the story writers who believed in God's interference with nature explained what had happened by saying that the sun had stood still, or perhaps Joshua himself had thought this. Yet, while modern believers reject that explanation of the event, they should accept the main point that is being made, namely, that it was God who enabled Joshua to gain the victory, and they will hold that the victory was due to God's giving Joshua and his men greater confidence, courage and endurance. The story is thus an example of how a true general pattern can be based on non-factual material.

A problem of a different kind is created by Mark's account of the calling of the first disciples. He tells how, as Jesus walked by the Sea of Galilee he saw Simon Peter and Andrew fishing from their boat, and called on them to follow him and become fishers of men, and 'straightway' they left their boat and followed him; a little later he saw the two sons of Zebedee mending nets with their father in his boat and called on them also, and they likewise followed him (Mark 1:16–20). To a modern reader it sounds as if all this happened within half an hour. What has to be realized is that Mark is giving a very compressed summary of a series of events – a general pattern without the details one would expect from a modern reporter. He does not mention that before the arrest of John the Baptist Jesus had done some preaching in Judaea beside the Jordan, and that with him there had been disciples who had baptized (John 4:2). These disciples presumably included Simon Peter and Andrew, who had previously followed John the Baptist (John 1:35–42). Thus what Mark describes is how Jesus told men who had already been with him that he was setting out on a new kind of mission, not baptizing but going to people in their villages, and how he asked them to join him; he had evidently decided on this form of mission after the arrest of John the Baptist. Here then we have a concise summary of a number of events, that is, a general pattern without the constitutive items people now expect.

The Nature of Truth

Most people today probably suppose that they know what truth is, but one often finds that Westerners fail to understand the complexity of truth. They have become very literal-minded, and assume that the only kind of truth is literal truth. In New Testament times people were not so literal-minded, and were often chiefly interested in symbolic truth. This can be illustrated from the Fourth Gospel. John gives great prominence to the changing of water into wine as the first of the 'signs' which Jesus performed. If this is understood literally as a physical change of water into wine, it has nothing to do with the gospel as understood by Christians, which is about the redeeming of human life and not the creating of drunkards. On the other hand, John placed it first because it was for him a symbol of what Jesus had achieved by his teaching and death and resurrection: he had changed something ordinary and humdrum into something rich and splendid, and this could apply both to the then current form of Jewish religion and to individual lives. *Only* when the changing of water into wine is understood symbolically is it the first of Jesus's signs.

John would also attach importance to the words of the master of the feast, 'You have kept the good wine until now', and would have understood these symbolically as describing God's dealings with his chosen people; and this would link up with the reform of the Jewish religion.

A further word may be said here about this event. It is not recorded in the other three gospels, perhaps because they doubted its factuality. The Authorized Version tells us how many firkins were involved, but we do not know what a firkin is. When we learn that the total amount of water changed into wine was something like 150 gallons, or 900 modern bottles, we begin to see the event differently. Even if a hundred people were present, that is nine bottles each. If they had already consumed as much or more, they were probably extremely fuddled. My personal view of the event is that the master of the feast was so drunk that he mistook the fresh cool water for a fine wine. This is still in a sense a changing of water into wine; it avoids the suggestion of interference with natural laws and yet fully accepts the point the evangelist is making.

There are instances where it is appropriate to speak about 'symbolic truth', but sometimes people think of the symbol as contrasted with the real thing it symbolizes, and thus in a sense unreal.[7] Because of this the word *symbolic* is best avoided in some religious discussions. There are similar difficulties with the words *metaphorical* and *analogical*. It was suggested above that the word *iconic* might be used, since an icon is a two-dimensional object which is accepted as a representation of a three-dimensional object although it is known to be inadequate. In some contexts the word *pictorial* may indicate something similar.

There is also some confusion about the word *literal*. There have been arguments recently in Scotland about the Virgin Birth and about whether Jesus is literally the Son of God. If 'literally' means 'in the primary sense of the word', then obviously Jesus cannot be literally the Son of God, because the transcendent God cannot physically father a child. Those who vigorously maintain that Jesus is literally the Son of God presumably mean that he is really and truly the Son of God; and, while I accept this, I would insist that it involves taking the word *son* in a secondary or iconic sense. God the Father is only something like a human father, and God the Son is only something like a human son.

From these considerations we may go on to look at a definition of truth, namely: the verbal or visual (pictorial) presentation of an aspect of reality is true when it presents that aspect as it is. This raises the question of how we know that reality is being presented as it is. In science and history there are various criteria that are widely accepted. In the sphere of religion I hold that, because language is being used iconically, the ultimate test is fruits. This also applies, however, in other fields. The ability to put men on the moon and bring them back again is a form of fruits, confirming belief in the truth of science. In history the wider patterns are concerned with the evaluation of events, and here a large part of the aim of the historian is to contribute to a picture of what is valuable, significant and important in this world in which people have to live. Such a picture influences the way in which they live their lives, and so bears fruits. Thus, while history has to take account of facts, it is more concerned with significance; and significance is an aspect of reality whose presentation is different from that of primary facts.

This may be illustrated from the infancy narratives in the First and Third Gospels. These are essentially ways of presenting the significance of Jesus, and the presentation of significance is not impaired even if some of the factuality is doubted. Most Christians are not aware that the two gospels seriously contradict one another. Matthew implies, without actually stating, that Joseph and Mary lived in Bethlehem; he says that shortly after the birth they went to Egypt, and only after spending some years there did they settle in Nazareth. Luke presents them as living in Nazareth and going from there to Bethlehem for the census, presumably about 24 December by our calendar; after the birth they remained in Bethlehem until 2 February, when they went to Jerusalem for Mary's purification and the 'redemption' of Jesus (after forty days), and after that they returned to Nazareth. This leaves no place for years in Egypt.

The existence of these contradictions between the two narratives shows that both cannot be factually true. The purpose of the narratives, however, is to present the significance of Jesus, and this means that there is little point in asking how much is factual. The probability is that, apart from the virginal conception itself, the statements of Matthew have little factual basis, though some of Luke's may have. In the First Gospel the coming of the wise men shows that Jesus has significance not only for Jews but also for the rest of humanity; and the conduct of Herod shows the opposition which divine truth has to face in the world. In Luke the words of Simeon and Anna in the temple are primarily expressions of the significance of Jesus, but all they may actually have said (if the incident occurred) is that this fine baby was sure to have a great future.

Difficulties have been raised about the virginal conception since there are no authenticated instances of this in human beings. With regard to its factuality I would say that, if it happened, it was not contrary to natural law but could possibly have come about through the intense spiritual experience Mary had when the angel visited her; but this would be in accordance with natural laws not yet known to science. The important point, however, is about the significance of the virginal conception. The absence of a human father has doubtless helped some Christians to think of Jesus as the Son of God, and many still seem to think that this is a proof of divinity. What few Christians realize is that 800 million Muslims also believe in the Virgin Birth or virginal conception, while firmly denying the divinity of Jesus. This should make it clear that virginal conception is in no way a proof of divinity. What it might be taken to show is that from the moment of conception Jesus was being prepared for the work he was finally to achieve.

I once heard a preacher comparing the nativity of Jesus to a modern girl having an illegitimate baby in a garage. For me this is a ridiculous, even blasphemous, example of the extent to which literal-mindedness can lead people astray. For one thing it is incorrect: Jesus was not an illegitimate child. Mary had not had physical contact with any human or even angelic male; and Joseph had taken her as his wife, and had fully accepted her child as his socially. They did not travel to Bethlehem as an unmarried cohabiting couple. The evangelist may have chosen the word translated *espoused* or *betrothed* to indicate that the marriage had not been consummated; but if they had not already been formally married, as Matthew states, Mary would not have needed to go to Bethlehem for the census. To suggest that Jesus is comparable to an illegitimate baby is a complete travesty of the gospel presentation of his significance for the world, as well as an implicit denial of the virginal conception, and shows how literal interpretations are misleading. The further suggestion that God was showing that he can use an illegitimate child has no basis in the work of the evangelists, even if God doubtless has this ability. For those who reject the virginal conception, the obvious alternative is to regard Joseph as the physical father of Jesus.

The two infancy narratives are primarily pictorial or iconic presentations of the significance of Jesus for the world. Because they enable people to understand something of this significance they are to this extent true. They are also an integral part of the total Christian system of belief, and should therefore be accepted as such. Since these narratives are pictorial or iconic in form, however, it is pointless to try to distinguish the factual in them from the non-factual. They should be accepted as they are, as being true, but 'without asking how' as the Muslims say.

Finally, there is the question of how religious presentations can be true when account is taken of the limitations of human language and thought, since these imply a degree of imperfection. From this standpoint there is certainly imperfection in religious assertions. I would maintain, however, that despite this there is a sufficient degree of truth in such assertions in the great religions to make them a satisfactory basis for living. They may be imperfect in some ways, but we have nothing better. As the Bible says, we cannot see God's face and live (Exodus 33:20; cf. John 1:18); and to see God's face is to have a complete knowledge of him. The Biblical presentation, however, of the realities of human life and of its dependence on God may be said to have been proved true by its fruits. For three millennia Jews and then Christians have been basing their whole lives on this presentation and have found that it works.

CHAPTER 3

Truth in the Old Testament

In former generations it was usually held by Christians that
the Bible was completely true, both Old and New Tes-
taments, but nowadays many of its assertions are being
seriously questioned. For this reason, and perhaps for others,
many Christians now tend to read only a few selected passages of the Old Testament and to neglect the rest. Yet the
Old Testament is an important part of our Christian heritage,
since the belief that Jesus was the Messiah foretold by Old
Testament prophets had a central place in early Christianity.
If, however, we are to have a fuller appreciation of the Old
Testament and its significance for Christians, there are many
problems about its truth which have to be looked at seriously.
This chapter is an attempt to deal with some of these.

The Evidence of Religious Development

Those who held that the Old Testament was wholly true
tended to assume that from earliest days the Hebrew people
had a full and adequate knowledge of God. Careful reading
of various passages, however, should have shown them that
this was not so, and that people like Jephthah (of whom more
will be said presently) had a clearly false conception. It was
realized, on the other hand, that there had been a development in people's understanding of what God required of
them, for in later prophetic books he was presented as giving
them a mission to the Gentiles.

Consideration of this question of development has been made more urgent and more difficult by the work of the literary critics during the last two centuries. The main results of their work are to be accepted, as is done, for example, in the notes and commentary of the Jerusalem Bible. An important point is that many of the books passed through a complex process of editing and re-editing. Each editor seems to have believed that he was justified in altering some of the details transmitted to him in order to make the general pattern more appropriate for his own time. This means that in the historical books there is evidence of how the Jews at the time of the final editing saw their past history, but no precise evidence of how the participants in the events saw them. In many cases, of course, it is possible to form a rough idea of how the participants felt, but this is based on inference and not on contemporary documentary material.

A further difficulty is that the world-view of both the participants and the editors was in some respects different from ours. One example would be their belief that the earth was flat, but this does not raise any problems. Mention has already been made of what is perhaps the most important point, namely, that God interferes with natural processes. There are numerous examples of this in the Old Testament, and in the New Testament Jesus is credited with a power of this kind.

It is to be noted, too, that some of the methods of the editors were different from those of modern scholars. When modern scholars find contradictory accounts of an event, they try to decide which is the more accurate and to follow it, or else they set forth both and say they cannot decide between them. In such cases, however, the Biblical writers often tried to conflate the two accounts into a single story, despite the discrepancies this contained. A good example of this procedure is the story of how Joseph was taken to Egypt (Genesis 37:12–36). One account is that, after the brothers had seized Joseph and were about to kill him, Reuben persuaded them instead to fling him into a dry well in the desert, hoping later to rescue him. While the brothers were some distance away, however, a passing caravan of Midianites found Joseph in the well, took him with them to Egypt and sold him there. Later Reuben went back to the well, found it empty and was greatly distressed. The other account is that, while the brothers were still thinking about killing Joseph, Judah saw a caravan of Ishmaelites passing and suggested that instead of killing him they should sell him to the Ishmaelites. The latter gave them twenty shekels and took Joseph to Egypt. In the text as we have it these two accounts have been fused into one. The first version is found in verses 21–5, 28a, 29–30 and 36, and the second in verses 25–7 and 28b. In this way we see that, when some details were not specially relevant to the general picture, the writer was content to leave inconsistencies. The general pattern was that because of the brothers' enmity Joseph was taken to Egypt, but the precise manner in which this came about did not matter.

This desire of the writers to preserve all that had come to them explains how they retained material they might have been expected to reject as unsuitable for their contemporaries. Such material makes it possible for us to form rudimentary ideas about the development of religion in the Old Testament period. There is much about God (Yahweh) strengthening the Hebrew leaders to give them victory in battle over their enemies. For at least some of the early leaders, however, this power that strengthened them was not the supreme God, but merely one god among many, even if he was perhaps more powerful than the others. This belief that there are many gods, though only one supporting the Hebrews, is found in the account of Jephthah's dealings with the Ammonites (Judges 11, especially verse 24). The latter were claiming some territory in Gilead and threatening to take it by force. In rejecting this claim Jephthah said that this territory had been given to the Israelites by their god, Yahweh, and that the Ammonites should be content with what had been given to them by their god, Chemosh. Jephthah presumably worshipped only Yahweh, but he believed that other gods existed.

The likelihood is that such a belief was widespread among the early Hebrews. In a psalm (95:3) constantly recited by Christians, it is stated that 'God is a great king above all gods'. Strictly speaking, this is an acknowledgement that there are other gods beside God; but I suspect that, when Christians recite it, they regard it as a poetic expression of God's greatness and do not take it literally.

Moses appears to have regarded Yahweh as the supreme God of the universe, since he held that it was he who had brought about the plagues which led to the Exodus of the Hebrews from Egypt. The later prophets mocked the powerlessness of the idols and contrasted it with the omnipotence of Yahweh. At the same time they were developing an understanding of what it meant for the Hebrews to be God's chosen people. To begin with this doubtless only meant that they were the people whom Yahweh supported; but in time it came to be realized that God expected the Hebrews not merely to worship him themselves but also to share the knowledge of him with the rest of the world. This was, for example, the message of the book of Jonah.

There is also evidence in the Old Testament of a development of moral ideas. In the earlier period God was believed to have given commands which to a modern person are barbaric. Joshua was commanded to put the population of various towns under the ban, and this meant that when they were defeated in battle, the whole population – men, women and children – were to be put to death. Even Moses is said to have ordered the death by stoning of a man who had broken the observance of the sabbath by picking up a few sticks to make a fire (Numbers 15:32–6). If the question is asked: Could the God and Father of our Lord Jesus Christ have issued such commands?, the modern Christian is inclined to answer no; but this would be wrong. The commands God gives to those who believe in him are relevant to the level of civilization in which they are living. We may deplore what was done to the towns in Palestine, but it was presumably appropriate under the social conditions of the time. When Moses ordered stoning, it was doubtless because a breach of sabbath observance by 'working' was thought to endanger the whole relationship of the Hebrews to God. What we have to learn from this is that there is moral development, and that not all the commands given by God in the distant past are appropriate to our day and generation. In the Mosaic law there was no rejection of polygamy, and it was practised occasionally by Jews into New Testament times and by some early Christians; but Christians have long rejected this.

There might also be said to be an element of moral development in the Hebrews' understanding of why God had chosen them. To begin with they perhaps accepted as a basic fact that they were the people God had decided to help, and this was beneficial for them and gave them more security. With the covenant on Sinai, however, it was becoming clear that God wanted them to be a community in which his justice was being practised. In the end they came to see themselves as a community which had the mission of conveying to the rest of humanity a fuller knowledge of God and of his commands for them.

The Great Truths of the Old Testament

In the light of the findings of the literary critics we can see the Old Testament not as a record of the religious experiences of Abraham, Isaac, Jacob and their descendants, but a record of these experiences as they were understood by the final editors of the various books. The central theme was how God had dealt with these people through the centuries. A modern person may wonder how they ever came to believe in God's activity in history. Abraham doubtless inherited some sort of belief in God and when he answered God's calls to him, felt that the results were satisfactory. Moses himself believed, and taught others, that it was God who had delivered them from serfdom in Egypt. The later prophets were convinced that God acted in history. These matters will presently be looked at in detail. Meanwhile the point to notice is that, once the Hebrew community had come to believe that God was active in human affairs, this became part of their world-view on which they based their lives, and commitment to this world-view proved satisfactory in practice. One could say that belief in God's activity in history was a theory which was tested out in practice by being made the basis of people's lives. There can indeed be suffering which the theory does not adequately explain; but the witness of the Jewish community right up to the present day, and the witness of the Christian community also, is that this theory works. It is supported by a vast amount of experience.

Let us now turn to consider the main truths the Old Testament writers found in their history and wanted to pass on to their contemporaries and successors. These may be described as the general patterns or pictures of divine activity which they wanted to present. It has been argued above that such patterns may be true, even if some of the details that constitute them are not entirely factual.

Did God choose Abraham?

Before trying to answer this question we should remember that owing to the limitations of human language God's choosing is only something like human choosing. We should also realize that we have no contemporary evidence. The two chief points to be considered are God's call to Abraham to leave his homeland, and his call to him to sacrifice his son. Let us commence with the second.

The modern Christian hesitates to accept the view that God called on Abraham to sacrifice his son only as a way of testing his obedience, not meaning him actually to carry out the sacrifice (Genesis 22). This does not fit in well with our conception of God. A possible alternative view of the facts would be that Abraham had inherited from his society a belief in God, but a belief in a God whose favour in critical situations had to be gained by human sacrifice. Presumably, then, in some threatening situation of which we are not informed, Abraham contemplated the sacrifice of his son Isaac, despite the fact that it was through Isaac that he hoped to have a progeny. The situation was so desperate, we may suppose, that he set about preparing for the sacrifice, but just before the final act he saw a ram caught in a thicket and took this as a sign from God that he was not to sacrifice Isaac. From this he went on to hold that the God he worshipped did not want human sacrifice. In this way Abraham became the representative of a new and higher conception of God. It is not necessary to suppose that God was directly responsible for the ram being in the thicket, but we should see Abraham's decision to abandon the sacrifice after he saw the ram as his acceptance of an inner voice from God.

The call to leave his homeland probably did not come out of the blue. In Iraq at that period there was a flourishing and expanding urban civilization based on arable farming, that of the Sumerians and then the Accadians. Because more land was being used for cultivation there was less for pasturing herds. This fact doubtless explains why Abraham's father Terah had left Ur in southern Iraq and moved to Haran in the north. With this urban civilization went authoritarian forms of rule which might have made it difficult for Abraham to maintain his religious beliefs. Because these material factors were present, however, that is no reason for denying that Abraham responded to an inner call which he believed came to him from his God. Abraham's response to this call and to the call to abandon human sacrifice put him in a position to hand on to his descendants a faith that was capable of developing into the Jewish and Christian religions. For this reason we are justified in holding that God did indeed choose Abraham. It should also be kept in mind that Abraham was not a solitary individual but the leader of something like a clan of nomadic pastoralists.

Did God bring about the Exodus from Egypt?

However much the story of the Exodus may have been rewritten in later times, the essentials presumably go back to Moses himself and his belief in God. He had been brought up by an Egyptian princess and given the best education of the day, but his heart was with his own people. When he killed an Egyptian who was attacking a Hebrew, he went into exile in Midian for some years. He could not forget, however, that the Hebrews were suffering a form of serfdom in Egypt and were being threatened with genocide by the killing of boy babies. Eventually he had an experience which led him to believe that God was calling on him to return to Egypt and work for the deliverance of his people. Although the Hebrews had been in Egypt over four hundred years, they had managed to retain something of Abraham's belief in God, and Moses shared in this belief.

We need not discuss here all the details, but must look in a general way at the ten plagues suffered by the Egyptians, which led to their permitting the Hebrews to depart. Apart from the tenth plague, the death of the first-born, these plagues were all natural occurrences, though perhaps of unusual severity. Moses himself is said to have believed that they had been specially brought about by God to make Pharaoh allow the departure of the Hebrews. He seems also eventually to have persuaded Pharaoh that this was so. Moses clearly thought in terms of the world-view of his time, but the modern believer does not need to suppose that God was interfering with the natural processes. The claims by Moses, however, to get God to put an end at a particular time to some of the plagues should probably be seen as a later rewriting of the facts.

The Hebrew crossing of the Red Sea (or Sea of Reeds) is depicted as miraculous, but is not necessarily so, and is again almost certainly later rewriting. There are said to be (or to have been) places where a large expanse of level sand was covered by water at high tide but not at low tide. Near Mont-Saint-Michel in France the tide is said to go out some fifteen miles and then to come in at the speed of a galloping horse. Even if something less than this happened where the Hebrews crossed, it would explain the incident. Moses may have had some knowledge of these local conditions after his journey to and from Midian, or he may have had some local informant. Such conditions would make it possible for the Hebrews to cross on dry land and then for the Egyptians, following a little later, to be caught by the tide. A high wind may also have contributed to the rise and fall of the water. Probably only a small detachment of the Egyptian army was involved and the disaster was not as extensive as the Bible suggests. There is no mention in the Egyptian records of any overwhelming disaster of this kind. Other incidents in the journeyings of the Hebrews are probably also susceptible of non-miraculous explanations.

If these conclusions are accepted, they imply that it was not through any miraculous or supernatural happenings that the Exodus came about and was successfully completed. God did not act in that way. What is obvious, however, is that the success of the initial Exodus and of the later travels was in large part due to Moses' strength of character, and this was something that was based on his belief in God. Thus, because God called Moses to work for the deliverance of the Hebrews and then gave him great strength of character throughout forty years, we are justified in saying that it was God who brought about the Exodus and carried it to a successful conclusion. In saying this we accept the general pattern of the Biblical writers as true, even though some of the details with which they constitute the pattern are not factual.

Did God choose the Hebrews and then the Jews?

Many scholars hold that the Jewish religion in something like its present form came into being as a result of the work of Ezra in about the middle of the fifth century BCE, and so from this period I speak of Jews. For the earlier period I have chosen to speak of Hebrews, though they are also called Israelites.

The next point we have to consider is the account of how God made a covenant with the Hebrews after their escape from Egypt, while they were at Mount Sinai (Exodus 19, 20, 24, 34, etc.). This was the 'old covenant' (of which 'old testament' is a variant and less accurate translation). God is also said to have made covenants with Noah, Abraham and other individuals, and that which he made with the Hebrews at Sinai may be regarded as a continuation of that with Abraham. God gave the Hebrews the Ten Commandments and many other detailed rules, and they promised to keep these and to worship him alone. In return God undertook to give them unparalleled support.

In all this, of course, God was acting through Moses and through the various inner promptings which Moses believed came to him from God. Thus the Biblical account of the Exodus and of the covenant must be derived from the statements made by Moses to the people and accepted by them. Moses presumably knew of the covenant with Abraham, but it was the voice of God speaking within him which made him think of a covenant with the entire Hebrew people and showed him the form it should take, namely, that the people should agree to obey the laws of God and worship him alone. In this way God through Moses made a covenant with the Hebrews, and in a sense chose them to be a special people for him. Such a choice (in so far as our human minds can comprehend it) was not arbitrary. The Hebrews, or at least some of their leaders, already had a truer knowledge of God than any of the surrounding peoples, and they were a community within which there were possibilities that this knowledge of God might be further developed.

The Hebrews sometimes seem to have thought of themselves as a people specially favoured by God for their own advantage, but eventually some of their prophets came to realize that God's choice of the Hebrews was not so much the conferring of a favour as the allocation of a task, namely, to develop the knowledge of God and communicate it to the rest of humanity. Once God's choice of the Hebrews and Jews is thought of in this way, it is possible to regard God as having assigned different tasks to the other great religions, so that each might develop aspects of the knowledge of God in ways for which its background fitted it.

Did God enable David to establish the kingdom?

David presumably accepted the belief of previous Hebrew military leaders that God helped them to victory in battle. This conviction would be strengthened by Samuel's anointing him with oil. It is, of course, expressed in the Psalms, but, while there is no reason to doubt that David composed psalms, it is clear that many of those in the book of Psalms were from writers in later centuries, and it is difficult to be certain which come from David himself. It is also clear, however, that David had great natural gifts as a military leader, and that these contributed to his final success in creating a very strong kingdom in the Middle East with several surrounding states paying tribute to it. There is no reason to doubt that it was God who enabled David to gain this great measure of success by strengthening him in various ways.

It is also appropriate here, however, to look at another incident in David's life, namely, his adultery with Bathsheba and his contriving the death of her husband. Muslims hold that all prophets are sinless, and they regard David as a prophet and deny the fact of his adultery. Yet the grounds for accepting the truth of this series of events are unassailable. The child of the adulterous union died, but Bathsheba's next son, after she married David, was Solomon who succeeded him. The point to seize on here is that those God chooses as instruments for his purposes are not always perfect. Indeed they are often imperfect, at least in minor ways. Yet God's purpose is achieved.

Did God send the great prophets?

The prophets whose books are found in the Old Testament from Amos onwards were primarily critics of the rulers and people of the two kingdoms of Judah and Israel. They were not primarily concerned with foretelling the future, though they did give warnings of disaster if people did not mend their ways in respect of both worship and conduct. The messages they brought fit well into what is known of the history of the kingdoms. They called on kings and people to observe a higher moral standard in social relationships. They attacked those who worshipped the fertility gods of the earlier inhabitants of the land, partly because lower moral standards were associated with these cults. They were often critical of the policies followed by the kings, especially when reliance on a foreign power replaced trust in God. Occasionally a king would ask the advice of a prophet about some future project. In all this there is nothing to suggest that the book-prophets and a few others were not inspired by God, and that in this way God sent them. There were numerous other prophets who fawned on the rulers and told them what they wanted to hear, but these are regarded as false prophets by the Biblical writers and we need not consider them further.

The difficult question is: When a prophet says that his message is the word of the Lord, is the message infallibly true? There is no difficulty about accepting as true, at least for their hearers, what they say about moral standards. Sometimes, however, when they prophesy destruction, it does not come about as they expect. The prophet Ezekiel, writing about the year 580 BCE when the Babylonians were besieging Tyre, the centre of a great trading empire, foresaw the imminent destruction of that city; but it survived the siege, and its empire continued for another two and a half centuries until the time of Alexander the Great. In the book of Jonah, when he prophesied destruction for Nineveh, the people of Nineveh repented and amended their ways, and God cancelled the destruction. There is nothing of this sort in the case of Tyre, however. What Ezekiel said would happen did not happen as he said it would. There are probably many similar cases in the prophecies directed against neighbouring states, but ordinary Christians do not notice them because they are ignorant of the historical background.

What then are we to say about such prophecies of disaster which were not fulfilled? The conclusion should probably be that, while the prophets were undoubtedly inspired by God, especially in their utterances about moral conduct and false worship, something of the prophet's own personality and intellectual outlook also came into the utterances, and the prophets were fallible men. Those whom God thus chose for his purposes were not always perfect in all respects. They could make mistakes in what we are perhaps entitled to consider secondary matters. To admit this leaves us free to maintain that in primary matters of morals and worship the messages were true and did indeed come from God. We should also regard as true the general principle underlying their statements about disasters, namely, that these come about as a punishment from God for sins of various kinds; where the prophets made mistakes was in matters of detail, which are secondary.

Did God bring about the Exile and the Restoration?

About 721 BCE an invasion by troops of the Assyrian empire (which had its capital in northern Iraq) finally put an end to the northern kingdom of Israel. Many of the leading citizens were deported to Iraq or elsewhere, while people from other countries were settled in and around Samaria (2 Kings 17). In 606 the Assyrian empire was brought to an end and replaced by a Babylonian empire (with its capital in central Iraq), which proceeded to attack the southern kingdom of Judah. Jerusalem was captured in 597 and some people deported to Babylon, including the king. Another king was put in charge of what was left of the kingdom, but after some years he rebelled. After a long siege Jerusalem had to surrender, the Temple was destroyed along with much of the city, and an end was made of the kingdom of Judah (587 or 586). There were more deportations, and only members of the poorer classes were left in the neighbourhood of Jerusalem (2 Kings 24, 25). These events were, of course, relatively small incidents in the history of the Assyrian and Babylonian empires. Each empire had a period of expansion when it covered a great area, and then a period of decline. The interest of these empires in Greater Syria, including Palestine, was due to this being a sphere of conflict between them and the Egyptian empire.

The first point to consider is whether, if the kingdoms of Israel and Judah had responded more positively to the prophets, they might have escaped destruction. The final fall of Judah came about because the king tried to free himself from the Babylonians by obtaining help from Egypt. The prophet Jeremiah warned him not to adopt this course, and called on him instead to trust in God. It is not impossible that, if the kingdom of Judah had responded to this call and had been content to live in relative isolation from its neighbours, the Babylonians might have left it alone or at least treated it less harshly. There is no certainty about this, however. This means that we cannot say that the Exile came about because of the failure of the people of Judah to respond to the later prophetic calls. The aggressive character of the Babylonians was such that the Exile might well have come about no matter how the Judaeans conducted themselves. Yet the experience of exile would have been less devastating, less of a disaster, if the Judaeans had learnt to trust more in God.

This being the situation, we have to ask in what way God may be said to have brought about the Exile. We cannot suppose that he did other than allow the Assyrians and Babylonians to follow their natural instincts. He did not inspire them to attack the kingdoms. It all happened in what might be called the natural or normal course of history. There was nothing arbitrary about it. What happened to the two kingdoms may be regarded as a normal consequence of the way they had been conducting their lives since their foundation in about 930 BCE. They had not confined themselves to their belief in God, but had accepted some of the political ideas of their neighbours. So God allowed the normal working out of these ideas among neighbouring peoples to teach his chosen people a lesson.

The great danger was that after such a catastrophe as the Exile the Hebrews would think that God had abandoned them or that their trust in God had been misplaced. By leading them to think of the Exile as a punishment from God, the prophets Jeremiah and Ezekiel enabled at least some of the exiles to retain their belief in God, and thus to be capable of recreating a state at Jerusalem when that became possible. By speaking of the Exile as a punishment the prophets were asserting that God was still in control of the historical process. In this case the instruments God was using were themselves ungodly and wicked, and the final overthrow of these powers bore out what the prophets said about the ultimate fate of such groups. The prophets were inspired by God to proclaim that the Exile was a punishment brought about by him, and we have no reason to doubt the truth of this.

The Restoration or return from exile began after the overthrow of the Babylonian empire by Cyrus the Persian in

O N E W O R L D
Books for Thoughtful People

If you wish to be placed on our mailing list, please return this card.
PLEASE PRINT

Name: _____

Address _____

City: _____ Nearest LSA (if any): _____

State (if U.S.A.): _____

Zip or Postal Code: _____ Country (if outside UK): _____

539. In the following year he issued a decree encouraging exiled Jews to return to Jerusalem and restore the Temple (Ezra 1:1–4). Cyrus was a Zoroastrian, that is, a member of a religion not unlike that of the Jews, though placing more emphasis on the powers of evil. With this religious position Cyrus was aware of the advantage of having his rule supported by the religions of the subject peoples. He may have given special consideration to the Jewish religion because of its similarity to his own. Isaiah (45:1) sees Cyrus as God's chosen instrument for the Restoration of the exiles, and we may accept this and see his religious policy as having come to him through the working of the Holy Spirit in his heart. There is thus no difficulty in seeing the Restoration as having been brought about by God. In actual fact there were enormous difficulties to be overcome. The first exiles to return (in 538) made a beginning, but not much was achieved until the arrival of a fresh body of exiles in 520. Even then things went slowly, and the restored community only became firmly established through the work of Nehemiah and Ezra in the middle of the fifth century BCE. The continuing support of God was an important factor contributing to the final success of the Restoration.

Has God still a mission for the Jews?

This question takes us beyond the Old Testament but it is appropriate to consider it here. The Christian Church originated in a body of Jews who believed that Jesus was the Messiah foretold by their scriptures. This implied that all other Jews had rejected the Messiah, and later Christians took this to mean that the main body of Jews had ceased to be God's chosen people; this status had been maintained, however, by those Jews who accepted the Messiah, and had then been shared with those non-Jews who joined them. The catastrophe of 70 CE could be seen as a fitting punishment for the rejection of the Messiah. Is this the only way of understanding these events?

Christians would certainly see the formation of the early Christian community, and its spread until it dominated the Roman empire, as having been brought about by God, and as a confirmation of their belief that they were his chosen people. It is Christian teaching that when a person called by God to do a piece of work fails at some point through sin and then repents, he or she is forgiven by God; and this forgiveness includes still having some work to do for God, though it may not be the same work as previously. This principle should certainly be applied to the Jews. Moreover in their case there were extenuating circumstances.

Jesus was not the Messiah most Jews were expecting, because he had reinterpreted the conception of the function of the Messiah. Many of the Old Testament references to the Messiah saw him as a Davidic figure leading his people to military victory (e.g. Psalms 2:9; 110:5,6); but there were also other conceptions of the Messiah, such as the suffering servant (Isaiah 42, 49, 50, 52–3) and the peaceful leader (Zechariah 9:9, 10). It was on these and similar passages that Jesus based the conception of the Messiah which he lived out, and he may also have understood the Davidic Messiah in a symbolic way. In a sense, then, what the Jews rejected was this conception of Messiahship, and this would seem to be less sinful; but the acceptance by many Jews of the false idea of the Messiah as a war-leader had much to do with the loss of their homeland in 70 CE. This could be seen as God's punishment for accepting the false idea. After that, however, some Jews may be said to have repented and to have been forgiven by God. The continuing existence of the Jewish community through the centuries could be taken as a confirmation that this is so, and that God still has a mission for them; but it is not for a Christian to say what precisely this mission is.

This examination of the main Old Testament assertions about God's activity in history shows that the central conception in them is true, namely, that God was behind the whole course of events from Abraham to the Exile and Restoration, directing and controlling what happened. The thought-world of the Biblical writers was very different from that of modern Western Christians, and to the latter many of the details of the Biblical stories sound like a fairy tale, something unreal. They cannot, for example, believe that the miracles of Elijah and Elisha (1 Kings 17 to 2 Kings 6) happened exactly as described, still less that Elijah ascended physically into heaven (2 Kings 2). In many such cases it is futile to speculate about the actual events out of which the story grew. The Biblical writers were ready to accept as factual many items modern Christians cannot accept as such, but the latter should see that this does not imply the false-hood of the general pattern the Biblical writers present of God's activity in history. Though modern believers certainly have to live in their own thought-world, perhaps they should realize that, unknown to them, it may have imperfections and even erroneous ideas. This should not, however, prevent them from believing in God's activity in historical events, primarily by calling, guiding and strengthening people, but possibly also in other ways. They may then see the strange stories as a kind of picture where only the general pattern is true, but at the same time they may find the details attractive in themselves.

If we regard the central Old Testament conception of God directing and controlling historical events as being roughly parallel to a scientific theory, then it has been amply verified by the experience of the Jewish and Christian communities over many centuries. People have lived on the basis of this belief and have found that it worked. It has had good fruits.

CHAPTER 4

Truth in the New Testament

Modern Biblical criticism has greatly changed our views about the New Testament. It has shown that the four gospels have been through complex processes of editing, not unlike various Old Testament books. While the gospels must go back to reports of people who had seen and heard Jesus, these reports may have been altered in some respects by later editors; for simplicity, however, the usual names of the evangelists are used here. Thus what we have in the gospels is a picture of Jesus as seen by Christians living a generation or more after the events. Scholars naturally want to know how much of the gospel reports can be considered the actual words of Jesus or a close reflection of them, and much work has been done on this. These are largely matters of detail, however, and do not raise general questions of religious truth, and so they will not be discussed further here. The other New Testament books also raise no general questions of this type. The discussion here will therefore be confined to the miracles, the resurrection and the assertion of the divinity of Jesus.

The Problem of Miracles

The early Christians, like other people of that time, believed that God could interfere with the ordinary course of nature. They also believed that similar unnatural or miraculous events could be brought about by human beings commissioned by God. Jesus is said to have believed that he cast out evil spirits 'by the finger of God', that is, by a divine power working through him. It was presumably also this same divine power which brought about similar acts in Old Testament times. Elisha, for example, was said to have raised a dead boy to life and to have fed a hundred men from twenty loaves (2 Kings 4).

The works of healing recorded of Jesus in the gospels present no real problem. He gave instruction to his disciples, and they also became capable of healing the sick and exorcizing evil spirits or, as we should say, curing mental illness. Healing was also practised in the early Church and, especially in the last half-century, a ministry of healing has been restored in many Christian bodies and even in some only on the fringe of Christianity. Such healing, then, is not to be regarded as interference with natural law. One might wonder if restoring dead people to life is also to be included among these works of healing. Jesus is reported to have brought back to life a widow's son in the village of Nain (Luke 7:11–15), and the daughter of an important man in Capernaum (Matthew 9:18–26; and parallels). In both cases the person was only dead for a short time, for in Palestine funerals traditionally took place within an hour or two of death. One wonders whether, with the limited medical knowledge of the times, a comatose state had been mistaken for death; if this was so, these instances would not be very different from the other works of healing. It is also possible that the evangelists were interested, at least in part, in the symbolism of bringing life to the spiritually dead – a point to be dealt with more fully in what follows.

Miracles other than the healings include the stilling of a storm and the feeding of thousands of people. In those cases the interpretation of the event as breaching natural law is probably due to the reporters and editors. On one occasion the disciples were in a boat with Jesus asleep when a storm arose; when they woke him, he is said to have ordered the wind and the waves to be calm. It would seem possible, however, that what happened was that the serenity and confidence of Jesus himself, once awake, communicated itself to the disciples and assuaged their fears; and then perhaps the storm suddenly subsided, as storms are said to do on the Sea of Galilee.

The accounts of the feeding of thousands with a few loaves and fish may be in part an attempt to show that Jesus was greater than Elisha. It would also seem to be the case, however, that these communal meals, if they can be so called, were in some sense a foreshadowing of the Eucharist, and that a small quantity of actual bread might have been a token of spiritual food. In the Fourth Gospel (chapter 6) the feeding of five thousand is linked by the writer with a Eucharistic discourse. There is also the possibility that many of those involved had brought food and that this was shared around.

It should also be kept in mind that the people of New Testament times thought symbolically more often than do our literal-minded contemporaries. This point was made in chapter 2. Both the stilling of the storm and the feeding of thousands may be understood symbolically, but it is in the Fourth Gospel that symbolic thinking reaches its peak. As was shown above, to speak of changing water into wine as the first of the 'signs' of Jesus only makes sense when it is understood symbolically as the changing of human lives. In a similar way John saw the raising of Lazarus from the dead (chapter 11) as a sign of the ability of Jesus to bring life to those who were spiritually dead. To emphasize this point he may have exaggerated the time Lazarus had spent in the tomb; but it is useless to speculate about the precise details.

Something was said above about the Virgin Birth or virginal conception of Jesus. The point was made there that part of the significance of virginal conception is that it tells us that from the moment of his conception Jesus was being prepared for his future mission. This was in line with the belief of the prophet Jeremiah (1:5) that God had been preparing him from the womb, and also with the belief expressed in one of Isaiah's servant-songs (49:1–5). Thus the Virgin Birth and infancy narratives can be accepted as true patterns or pictures of the significance of Jesus, despite doubts about the factuality of all the details; and their importance, when so understood, is that they are presentations of religious truth.

The Resurrection of Jesus

Jesus was crucified on a Friday, and his body was laid in a tomb before the sabbath began at Friday sunset. When disciples went to the tomb on Sunday morning they found it empty. The Christian calendar is based on the view derived from Luke's Gospel (24:49–52) and Acts (1:3) that Jesus appeared to groups of disciples on a number of occasions during the next forty days, that on the fortieth day he ascended into heaven to the right hand of God, and that on the fiftieth day the Holy Spirit came down on the disciples and other believers. There are divergences from this view, however, in other gospel accounts.

In the Fourth Gospel (20:22) it is stated that the disciples (apart from Thomas) received the Holy Spirit at the first appearance of Jesus to them, although it also speaks of later appearances. Other divergences are whether the first appearances were near Jerusalem or in Galilee, and whether the stone closing the tomb had been rolled away before the women arrived on Sunday morning, or whether it was still in place but was moved away by an earthquake after their arrival. There are also several other points of this kind. To the modern historian these divergences are not a reason for rejecting the accounts, because it is normal to find that when many people report an event they do so in slightly different terms. In the case of the resurrection of Jesus a great many people were involved, for Paul describes an appearance to over five hundred people.

The most certain fact behind all the accounts is that a profound change took place in the lives of large numbers of the followers of Jesus. From being utterly dejected and dispirited after the crucifixion, they became full of joy and happiness, with a sense of having been witnesses of a triumph of good over evil, and of now being entrusted with the task of sharing this with others. Their accounts of the appearances to them of the risen Jesus were their attempts to explain how the change in their lives had been brought about. All this is solid fact.

Another fact is that the tomb was found empty, but this does not really prove anything since, as was realized at the time, the body could have been stolen by robbers. It is also a fact that there was no corpse anywhere. Had the disciples known of it they could not have preached resurrection, and had their opponents known of it they would have produced it to refute the preaching. The disciples thought that what appeared to them was the physical body of Jesus, and on some occasions they saw him eating food; but it was not exactly a physical body, because it could come into a room with closed doors and could vanish into thin air. Moreover their belief in the resurrection of Jesus was more than an inference from his appearances to them, for he had not simply been restored to temporal life but was somehow in eternal life; there was no suggestion that he might be rearrested.

It also appears to be the case that in the appearances the followers of Jesus were somehow being taught. The clearest example of this is the story of the two disciples walking to Emmaus (Luke 24:13–32); when Jesus appeared to them he taught them that his passion and death were not a disaster but the proof of his Messiahship. In all the appearances, too, those present were made to feel not just that Jesus was alive but that he was gloriously alive.

According to the Church's calendar, Jesus ascended into heaven on the fortieth day to be seated on the right hand of God. This is not something that the disciples observed. There is indeed a report that Jesus led the disciples to the Mount of Olives and there was taken up from them into heaven; but this is heaven in the sense of 'sky'. One does not reach the heaven where God dwells by going upwards, however far; one only reaches the moon or Mars. The ascension is something that takes us beyond the world of space and time and what is observable. It was a corollary of the disciples' coming to believe that Jesus was the Messiah, because God had said to the Messiah, 'Sit on my right hand' (Psalm 110:1).

If it was impossible for the body of Jesus to reach heaven by going in an upward direction, what happened to it? This is a mystery to which we are unable to give a solution. The followers of Jesus thought that the body which appeared to them was identical with the body which had been laid in the tomb, but it had been changed into what scholars have called the 'resurrection body', which could suddenly appear and suddenly vanish. And what happened to this resurrection body? Did it just stop appearing? There is no satisfying answer to these questions. This is another place where we must hold that the general pattern, resurrection to eternal life, is true, while having no clear knowledge of the details which constitute it. It has also to be remembered that human beings are thought to be capable of entering into eternal life without their physical bodies.

We usually think of eternal life as life continuing indefinitely, but this is an inadequate conception, since our minds cannot fully grasp the reality. Eternal life is only something like spatio-temporal life going on endlessly, though for many purposes this is an adequate way of thinking about it. Eternal life may also be described as life or existence in a higher sphere of being beyond time and space, where one is in some sense with God. The promise of eternal life to believers cannot be verified in this present life, but those believers who achieve some awareness of God's presence with them in this life can look forward with assurance to what lies beyond.

The Divinity of Jesus

Before we consider how the first followers of Jesus came to think of him as divine, it is helpful to look at the Old Testament conception of the relation between humanity and divinity, since this is different from what most people today suppose it to be.

In the account of the creation of human beings it is said

that God made them in his own image, both male and female (Genesis 1:26f; 5:1f). This statement has several implications. One is that there is something of the divine in each human being, perhaps intelligence and awareness of what is meaningful, together with a capacity for love. It would also seem to follow that in creating the world and controlling its history God foresaw a consummation in which the human race would share. The picture of the New Jerusalem (Revelation 21) is an attempt to suggest what this might be. It is also the case that the world has been made a place in which it is possible for human beings to have pleasant and meaningful lives, even if sometimes there are natural catastrophes like earthquakes; most of the suffering of human beings comes from other human beings. Finally, there must be in God what might be called a human or anthropic aspect, even if the human qualities we ascribe to him, such as intelligence, wisdom, purpose and love, are only something like what these are in human beings.

Next it must be noticed that there are a number of places where the Old Testament speaks of God as a father and of human beings as his children. Isaiah (43:6) pictures God as saying to north and south, 'Bring my sons from far and my daughters from the ends of the earth'; and Jeremiah (31:19) reports God as saying 'I am a father to Israel and Ephraim is my firstborn'. These two verses are apparently referred to by Paul (2 Corinthians 6:18). In another passage Jeremiah speaks of the kingdoms of Israel and Judah as faithless wives whom he hopes will return to God and call him 'My father'; and he also speaks of God's children (3:6–22). At various points in the Old Testament the expected Messiah from David's descendants is spoken of as God's son. 'He shall cry to me, "You are my father, my God, the rock of my salvation";

I will make him my firstborn' (Psalm 89:26). 'He said to me, "You are my son, today I have begotten you" ' (Psalm 2:7). The phrase 'son of God' is not used in these passages, although it is implied, but sonship does not mean that the person is divine, only that he has been given a special task by God while remaining completely human.

In the century before Jesus the phrase 'son of God' is said to have come into use to denote the expected Messiah. Where the phrase occurs in the gospels, we cannot be sure whether it was actually used in the time of Jesus or has been introduced later in the writing of the gospels. What can be said is that, if it was used in the time of Jesus himself, it meant no more than the special human agent of God; it could not have meant the second hypostasis of the Trinity.

This is the background against which we have to understand how the first followers of Jesus, who had known him as a human being like themselves, came to think of him as also divine. The basic answer, I would hold, is clear. They thought of Jesus as divine because of what he had achieved as Messiah. The difficulty is to state in words what precisely this achievement was. It was not what was commonly expected of the Messiah, such as deliverance from the Romans, because Jesus had reinterpreted the conception of Messiahship. What then was it that he had achieved?

Jesus is commonly spoken of in the New Testament as the one who redeems and saves, as having redeemed the human race and brought it salvation; and in the Old Testament there are many references to God as redeeming and saving. It was also known from the Old Testament, however, and emphasized by Jesus, that God forgives sins; but it would seem that many Jews were not convinced by a mere statement to this effect. It was difficult for them to believe that the guilt of their sins had been completely cancelled. Thus John the Baptist came calling on people to repent of their sins, but he also introduced the symbol of baptism to show that the guilt of their sins had been washed away.

A slightly different picture is given by Paul in his second letter to the Corinthians (5:18f):

> All things are of God, who has reconciled us to himself by Jesus Christ, and has given to us the ministry of reconciliation, namely, that God was in Christ reconciling the world to himself, not imputing their trespasses to them, and has committed to us the word of reconciliation.

The most important words here are probably that 'God was in Christ'.

Yet another way of looking at the achievement of Jesus is by considering the idea of a new covenant. This had been spoken of by Jeremiah (31:31–4) and other Old Testament prophets as the initiation of a new and deeper relationship between God and human beings; all were to have a direct knowledge of God. Jesus seems to have taken up this idea and at the Last Supper spoke of his blood as the blood of the new covenant; and he is called the 'mediator of a better covenant' in the Epistle to the Hebrews (8:6).

These different ways of speaking of the achievement of Jesus are to be regarded as complementary, since he did achieve all the things described and more. It was from these that the early Christians went on to think of Jesus as divine. In the Old Testament it was God who redeemed and saved, and Paul had gone so far as to say that 'God was in Christ reconciling the world to himself'. After Jesus had been accepted as the suffering Messiah, verses from the Psalms could be applied to him, especially that verse where God tells him to sit on his right hand. It should be noted, however, that ascension into heaven does not imply divinity, for Elijah also had been taken up into heaven; and even sitting at the right hand of God was probably not at first taken as signifying divinity.

The fullest expression of the New Testament understanding of the divinity of Jesus is in the opening verses of the Fourth Gospel. John there identifies Jesus with the Word of God. By this we should understand what was called above the human or anthropic aspect of God. The Greek word *logos* suggests primarily intellect, but moral qualities were clearly also involved, especially God's outgoing love for humankind. John further speaks of the Word of God as participating in the creative process by which the world has come into being, and in the book of Genesis that process may be seen as a manifestation of the human aspect of God. Finally John says that the Word became flesh, that is, a human being, and lived among us.

From this we go on to ask how Jesus in his human life differed from other saintly persons. Many of the great saints, especially towards the end of their lives, may be said to have been fully responsive to the inner promptings which came to them from God. Jesus also would receive such inner promptings and would respond, but the final series of promptings were of a different character, and it was the response to these which led to his passion and death. They were essentially a call to a course of action which would express a new and deeper conception of God's outgoing love for human beings; but this conception could not be adequately presented in any form of teaching; it had to be demonstrated by being lived out in a human life, and that is what Jesus did. We thus see in the closing weeks of the human life of Jesus a perfect manifestation of God's love for his creation. God was more fully present in this human life than he had ever been present in any human life. Here was the human aspect of God in its fullest expression.

There is also a sense, of course, in which God has been present in the lives of the saints and of people like Moses and Muhammad. Through these two in particular he brought about an important degree of the fulfilment of his purposes for human life. The difference between them and Jesus is in respect of what I have called the achievement of Jesus. This achievement is something which, like the nature of God, it is impossible to express fully in human words. As has already been said, the various names for it, such as the salvation of the world, redemption from sin and the mediation of a new covenant, are complementary, and none is exhaustive. Christians claim, however, that this achievement is unique and that there is nothing exactly like it in any of the other great religions. It is because of the uniqueness of the achievement of Jesus that there is also a uniqueness in his relationship to God.

The New Testament writers seem to have been beginning to understand the phrase 'son of God' as indicating the unique position of Jesus. They also speak occasionally of Father, Son and Holy Spirit, and this suggests that a conception of the threefoldness of God was taking shape in their minds. At the same time, however, they held that those who believed in the uniqueness of Jesus were themselves children of God. As John put it, 'as many as received him, to them gave he power to become the sons of God' (John 1:12). While the sonship of Jesus was held to be unique, it was not always clear how it differed from that of Christian believers. Sometimes they were said to be sons by adoption, but elsewhere Jesus was called the firstborn of many brethren – a phrase which would link up with his achievement as inaugurating a new and deeper relationship between God and human beings.

Many Christians when they pray have a picture of Jesus before their minds and feel that this brings them into the presence of God. This is altogether appropriate, and is an important confirmation of belief in the divinity of Jesus; but by itself it should not be taken as a proof. Hindus in their prayers may have a picture of Krishna before them, and feel that this brings them into the divine presence; but this is hardly an argument for the divinity of Krishna.

The Threefoldness of God

Although trinitarian doctrine as it has come to us is largely the work of the ecumenical councils of the fourth and fifth centuries, it is appropriate to consider it here, since it rounds off and stabilizes the ideas towards which the New Testament Christians were moving. By the time of these councils the majority of Christians were from a Gentile background, and the doctrine was worked out in terms derived from Greek philosophy. For this reason the formulations were rejected by Christians from a Jewish background.

The first remark to be made is that, if Christians today want to understand the doctrine of the Trinity, they should abandon the English word *person* and stop speaking about three persons in one substance. This is not because of any change in the doctrine, but because the English word *person* has changed in meaning since it was first used in the sixteenth century to translate the Latin *persona*. The predominant meaning of *person* now is an individual human being, and the Trinity is not even something like three individual beings, still less a select society of three. The word *persona* which was used in the Latin version meant firstly an actor's mask (through which sound came) and then a role in a play. There is much to be said for holding that God has three roles, and perhaps one might also venture to speak of three aspects.

It is worth remarking here that *person* is by no means the only word that has changed its meaning since the sixteenth century. The Holy Ghost is not what people now mean by a ghost; and when the Church of England prays that God will 'prevent us in all our doings with [his] most gracious favour', it means almost exactly the opposite of what *prevent* now means (Collect after Holy Communion; see also collects for Easter Day and Trinity XVII).

Not much reflection is needed to see that there are three main ways in which divine activity affects human beings: (1) God created us, each one individually, and put something of his being into us, since we are made in his image; (2) in the life and death of Jesus there was perfectly embodied a fuller revelation of the outgoing love of God for human beings; and (3) throughout history God has been working in human hearts, guiding and strengthening them, and this has happened even where the persons so acted upon did not believe in God and did not know that he was working in them. (The creed makes it clear that the Holy Spirit was active before Pentecost, because it asserts that he spoke through the prophets.)

It would be wrong, however, to think that these three roles or forms of activity are neatly marked off from one another. The passion and death of Jesus may be seen as the consummation of the Father's redemptive activity; and the Fourth Gospel speaks of the Word of God as participating in the creative process, so that it is through him that all things have been made. The distinction between the second and third forms of activity also seems to be blurred in the New Testament. Paul can say, 'The Lord is the Spirit' (2 Corinthians 3:17); and also that 'I live, yet no longer I, Christ lives in me' (Galatians 2:20), although one would expect this indwelling divine presence to be called the Holy Spirit. Thus the precise way in which God is threefold is not altogether clear. In the present multi-religious situation, however, when Christians have frequent contacts with members of other faiths who believe in God's oneness, it is important that they should be able to explain the different ways in which they see God as affecting human lives and, also and above all, their belief in the oneness of God.

CHAPTER 5

God in the Other Religions

After the consideration of some general aspects of religious truth and a closer look at specific problems regarding Biblical truth, I turn now to discuss questions about the truth found in other religions. What I have to say is based on the belief that God has been active in some way in all the main religions of the world. I would agree that this is in a sense a theory; but I would maintain that it accounts better for the phenomena than any other view or theory. God's activity in the various societies, of course, is always related to the world-view of the society and to its stage of development. God's revelation of himself is limited by deficiencies in the world-view, and it also requires individuals with a capacity for becoming aware of God's messages through their inner promptings. There is no reason to suppose that the activity of God will ever cease so long as there are imperfections in human society requiring correction. The Muslim dogma that there will be no prophet after Muḥammad may be accepted in the sense that there will be no revelation of a complete new religion; but it would seem certain that it is open to God to give messages of a revelational character to individuals within the existing religions where these religions are in need of improvement or correction.

The activity of God in all the main religions, however, does not mean that they are all completely true. They are partly based on human responses to divine initiatives, and these responses may contain imperfections. Moreover, as has been pointed out, the limitations of human thought and language mean that the comparison of religious assertions at a purely intellectual level is not always helpful. The essential criterion for the degree of truth to be found in a religion, when considered as a whole, is its fruits in the life of its adherents.

The Beginnings of Religion

To hold that not merely is there something of God in each human being, but also that God may be active, at least potentially, in each human life, is in accordance with the Old Testament belief that human beings are made in the image of God. Doubtless some people are much more open to God's activity than others, more aware of it and more responsive to it, but such people will describe their experience in different ways. One person may say that God or an angel spoke to him or her. Another may feel a strong impulsion to act in a certain way. For others the main experience may be of a presence of God with them. For these and other forms of experience of divine activity I use the term 'inner promptings'. In Christianity inner promptings of different kinds are ascribed to the Holy Spirit.

A religion presumably begins when people who have had an inner prompting think they have something to share with their neighbours. How they describe to their fellows the outcome of their inner prompting depends on the culture in which they live, and more particularly on the world-view. The description must make sense to the hearers. Doubtless at the beginning of a religion what is asserted may be crude and imperfect, but from this beginning something better may be developed as further inner promptings are received.

It is conceivable, of course, that a person might think an inner prompting came from a divine source, when it was no more than an urge from his or her own unconscious, and in such cases the religion might be definitely bad.

In considering the early stages of a religion the important question to ask is not whether what was asserted was true, but what the fruits were in the lives of those who accepted the assertions as a basis for living. Because religious language is not precise but only tells us that what we worship is something like this or that, it follows that no religious assertion can be said to be unequivocally true, though it might sometimes be possible to say that an assertion is unequivocally false. It is also, of course, the case that, though the assertions are based on inner promptings from God, they may be imperfect in many ways. In early times the world-view of a culture was inadequate at various points, and that determined the precise form of the assertions. Even if there were some imperfections in these, however, there would also be a measure of truth, and that would enable people who followed them to lead better lives; in other words they might still have some good fruits. Belief in a flat earth, for example, if implicit in the commands, would be unlikely to have social consequences, good or bad.

Early religion, in addition to assertions about the nature of the world in which people lived and the forces controlling it, usually also contained divine commands for the guidance of human conduct. It was seen above in connection with the Old Testament that these commands are always suited to the social forms existing in a community and, more generally, to the level of civilization to which it has attained. Over the centuries communities change and develop in various ways, and this makes changes in the religion also desirable. Each generation grows into the religion of the previous generation, and, if this is proving unsatisfactory in some ways, one or more individuals may receive inner promptings leading to an improvement of the unsatisfactory features. Just as the Old Testament religion progressed from the crude monolatry of Jephthah and the barbaric actions of Joshua to the prophetic vision calling the Jewish people to share with the rest of humanity their insights into the true being of God, so there have been comparable developments in the other great religions. Behind all these should be seen the activity of God, and from this it follows that God has a task for each religion, though one appropriate to its social milieu.

Some of these points may be illustrated from the Old Testament where it refers to other contemporary forms of religion. The prophets fiercely attacked the idols of the earlier inhabitants of Palestine because many people in the kingdoms of Israel and Judah tended to turn to them. The prophets make fun of the idols and emphasize their power-lessness, but this is no more than an *argumentum ad hominem*. The main idols attacked were the Baals and Ashtoreths (Astartes), that is, male and female fertility deities, but these represent real and important powers in the world. Without the fertility of human beings and the fertility of animals and crops, life would become extinct. Fertility also means male and female sexuality. The worship of these deities was linked with a world-view which emphasized the reality of sexuality as a power with some control over human life, and also as a source of meaningful experience. In many of the temples there was a tradition of sacral prostitution. Along with the emphasis on sexual satisfaction there went a lack of emphasis on justice. This is illustrated by the story of

Naboth's vineyard. Jezebel, the wife of King Ahab of Israel, was from the Baal-worshipping family of the king of Sidon. When Naboth refused to sell his ancestral vineyard to the king, Jezebel hired men to bring false charges against him and have him stoned to death; and in this wicked way she procured the vineyard for Ahab (1 Kings 21).

Had such a religion any genuine fruits? We have no information about the lives of ordinary people in Sidon, for example, and can only guess at the fruits. Presumably some people, especially men, were able to have a more or less satisfactory life. We know, however, that some of our contemporaries who devote much time to the pursuit of sexual pleasure tend to lose all appreciation of deeper forms of meaningful life; and something of this sort was doubtless true of the more successful in a place like Sidon. Presumably, however, there were many there who had little sexual satisfaction and many who suffered from injustice. For reasons not necessarily connected with the religion, there would be a degree of social stability which would help to make life tolerable for most people. On the whole, however, it would seem that the fruits of a fertility religion were at most only moderately good.

The worship of Baal and Ashtoreth may seem to be a long way from our present-day world, because we do not go in for metal and wooden idols. Yet an increasing number of people in many parts of the world believe that the physical satisfaction of sex is the supremely meaningful experience in human life. Though there are no images, a greatly admired person may be spoken of as a sex-idol. Perhaps we should be enlarging our conception of religion to give a place to such manifestations of modern life. Yet they do not seem to lead to the cohesion seen in religions in the past, and that makes it difficult to know how to deal with these manifestations.

Another form of worship described in the Old Testament is that of the golden image set up by Nebuchadnezzar (Daniel 3). This image represented the power inherent in the structure of the Babylonian empire and in the person of the emperor. Again this was something completely real which ensured the relative well-being of thousands of people. It probably had many defects, but at least it had some good fruits.

Some of the forms of worship in the Roman empire, such as the worship of the emperor and of *Dea Roma*, seem to have been similar. The empire provided a high degree of social stability over a large area, as Nebuchadnezzar's had probably also done. We know further that Rome had a good record for seeing that all its people were justly treated. Paul was proud to be a full citizen of the Roman empire. To this extent the imperial religion of Rome had good fruits. We know, however, from the New Testament and other contemporary sources that there was a considerable measure of spiritual starvation, and that many people were looking for a religion which would enable them to live a more meaningful life.

It might be appropriate after this reference to the worship of imperial power to say a word about a modern phenomenon, namely the adulation of Hitler in Germany and the movement of so-called German-Christians. Even apart from the latter there were many observances of a religious character, such as vast concourses of people engaged in what amounted to the worship of Hitler. This worship presumably grew out of the inner promptings of numerous people, but such promptings came largely from the seamier side of their human nature, and so approved the evil practices and policies of the regime. The German-Christians may have retained some true ideas from genuine Christianity, but they had combined these with objectionable promptings from a human source. Once the criterion of fruits is applied to this religion or quasi-religion it stands condemned.

Culture and the Religions

The beginnings of the great religions are lost in the mists of history. Abraham is dated about 1800 BCE, but already there seems to have been some sort of religion for him to inherit or grow into. It is impossible to say how far back we have to go to reach the first religious inner promptings. Almost certainly these promptings came at a time when the human race consisted of a large number of relatively isolated cultural units, each slightly different from its neighbours and having few contacts with them. Occasionally, where the terrain favoured it, political power was able to create larger units. This was the case in Egypt, Iraq and parts of India and China. In these larger units there was presumably some merging of previously diverse local cults.

It seems probable that, to begin with, a religion would achieve little acceptance except in the culture in which it originated, since it would be attuned to the needs and thought-forms of this particular culture. Where there was a merging of cultures there might be some merging of religions, but it is also possible that one religious form managed to suppress the others. There would sometimes also be an association of religion with political power, where religion helped the latter to bring about a merging of cultures. The merged cultures were not necessarily monolithic, for elements from some of the submerged cultures might have managed to maintain themselves.

What seems to be true, however, is that in the world up to the seventeenth century or so, each of the great religions had established itself in an area of its own, and that in this area (which might be nearly a quarter of the inhabited world) there was a distinctive culture closely linked with the religion. There were a few regions where there was some intermingling of religions, but on the whole, even in such regions, there were few contacts between the adherents of the different religions except at a purely mundane level.

Against this background it may be helpful to look at the early history of the relation between the Christian religion and various cultures. Christianity originated within Jewish culture, and this was a culture which was trying to maintain a degree of individuality against the invasive pressure of the predominantly hellenistic culture of the surrounding world. By the time of Jesus Palestine had become part of the Roman empire which, especially in its eastern provinces, was largely hellenistic in culture. Many Jews had become romanized or hellenized, in much the same way as in recent times many of the upper classes in Third World countries have become westernized. At that time there was a kind of religious vacuum in the Roman empire. There was some worship of imperial power, and that was having good fruits, but it did not satisfy all the people's religious needs. From the book of Acts in the New Testament we know that attached to the Jewish synagogues which were to be found in many of the cities of the eastern empire there were groups of 'those who feared God', that is, non-Jewish persons seeking some deeper awareness. It is not clear why such persons did not become Jews. Perhaps, for example, the men among them feared the painful process of circumcision; but it is also possible that, although allowed to be present at worship in the synagogues, they did not feel fully accepted by the Jewish community. If such persons had become Jews, then Judaism might eventually have become the official religion of the Roman empire, and the subsequent history of the world might have been different.

What in fact happened was that these 'God-fearers' were welcomed into Christian communities, largely through the work of the apostle Paul. They were not required to be circumcised and they were fully accepted as fellow-believers. In the course of time these Gentile or non-Jewish believers within the Christian Church greatly outnumbered the believers from a Jewish background. They were persons whose culture was basically hellenistic, and in the ecumenical councils of the fourth and fifth centuries they voted for expressions of Christian belief in terms of Greek philosophical concepts, which were unacceptable to persons from other cultural backgrounds. Some small communities of Christians from a Jewish background maintained their existence in isolation from the main body of the Church.

More important, however, were four bodies of believers who were labelled as heretics by the ecumenical councils. These were the Copts, the Syrian Jacobites, the Nestorians and the Armenians. Each of these bodies had a distinctive religious language, and it would seem that each consisted of people who, though partly hellenized, also retained something of an older culture. The Copts are the descendants of the ancient inhabitants of Egypt, and they retained something of the deep interest in eternal life which in earlier ages had led to the building of pyramids. The Armenians, who were condemned as heretics at a later date, have continued until today to use their own language. The other two bodies used different forms of Syriac, and were at different poles theologically, though perhaps not so clearly marked off from their neighbours as the Copts and Armenians.

By declaring these bodies heretical the ecumenical councils were trying to impose from above, as it were, a purely hellenistic culture, and it was this that was resisted. The whole series of events shows that the leaders of the Church at the time were unable to find a solution to the problem of cultural diversity. It is possible that their treatment of 'heretical' bodies led to a weakening of Christianity in those regions which were to come under Muslim rule in the seventh century; but there never seems to have been more than a small trickle of converts from these bodies to Islam.

In the eleventh century the separation of the Eastern Orthodox Christians from the Western Catholic Christians was probably also due in part to cultural factors. The Latin-speakers in the west of the Roman empire were never so interested in philosophical matters as the Greek-speakers in the east. The separation of the Protestants at the Reformation doubtless also owed something to cultural differences.

God in Islam

To give more substance to the general statements about the activity of God in the non-Christian religions I shall now deal in some detail with the workings of God in Islam as I have come to understand them.

Many of the earlier Christian scholars who wrote about Islam in Greek and Latin were aware both that the Qur'ān denied some basic Christian truths, such as the divinity of Jesus, and also that it had many references to Biblical characters such as Noah, Abraham and Moses. Because of its denials they saw it as a false religion, and they concluded that it had been patched together by Muhammad from reminiscences of Biblical stories. One of the forms of apologetic against this view adopted by Muslim scholars was to hold that the word *ummī*, which is applied to Muhammad in the Qur'ān, means 'illiterate', so that Muhammad could not have read the stories in the Bible but must have received them by revelation from God. *Ummī* probably originally meant 'Gentile' or 'non-Jewish', but apart from this the argument from Muhammad's illiteracy is feeble, since he could have found someone to read the Bible to him or to recount the stories.

Recently I was asked to write an article on 'Islamic Attitudes to Other Religions',[8] and, when I looked carefully at what the Qur'ān had to say about other religions, I was astounded to see how little knowledge there was of the central truths of Judaism, and how virtually nothing was known about Christianity apart from the Virgin Birth and the assertion of the divinity of Jesus. The Biblical stories referred to in the Qur'ān are mainly from the books of Genesis and Exodus, and there are additions which are sometimes from extra-Biblical Jewish sources. Thus there are many accounts of parts of the life of Moses, but several of these are about his arguments with Pharaoh and his magicians, and there is no clear statement that the great work of Moses was to deliver the Israelites from a state of near slavery in Egypt and to bring them eventually through difficult terrain to the land promised to their ancestors by God. For Moses and other early Biblical characters, with the exception of Joseph, the Qur'ān tends to relate incidents in isolation, and does not show how they are related to one another within the person's career. The reader familiar with the Bible has no difficulty in seeing these incidents as part of a connected story, but from the Qur'ān alone it would be difficult to see how they fit together, since some central incidents are completely omitted, such as Abraham's call to leave his homeland.

To sum up: the Qur'ān does not make clear that what Moses achieved was to deliver his people from slavery in Egypt and bring them to the borders of Palestine; it has nothing about the settlement in Palestine; it mentions David as a prophet who received a scripture, the Psalms, but not as a victorious general who created a powerful kingdom; it has nothing about this kingdom and its division into two; it has nothing about the great prophets who criticized the kings and their people; it has nothing about the Exile and Restoration. In short, there is nothing about what Jews would regard as the basic history of their religion, the history which justifies their belief that God has supported the Jews. If this represents the position in Mecca and in Muḥammad's own mind about knowledge of the Jewish religion, then it would seem to follow that the profound knowledge shown by the Qur'ān of many truths about God's being must have come to Muḥammad by divine inspiration. This would support Muḥammad's own declaration that the Qur'ān was not the product of his conscious mind, but came to him from beyond himself, a declaration which non-Muslims must evaluate. The different 'manners of revelation' recorded by Muslim scholars are presumably the ways in which Muḥammad at different times experienced the receiving of revelations from God.

In other words, Muhammad was a prophet comparable to
the Old Testament prophets, though his function was somewhat different. The latter were primarily critics of deviations
from an existing religion, whereas he had to bring knowledge of God and of his commands to a people without any
such knowledge. In this respect Muhammad's role and station more closely resembled that of Moses in that through
each of them a form of the divine law was communicated to
their people, although Moses is spoken of in the Bible as
law-giver, not as prophet.

Non-Muslims should also see the hand of God in the
spread of Islam to many Arab tribes during the lifetime of
the prophet. There was a religious vacuum here which the
message of the Qur'ān filled, a vacuum which both Judaism
and Christianity had been unable to fill except to a slight
extent. There were Jewish groups in Medina, but they had
achieved little by way of converting the Arabs to belief in
God. There were Christian clans and tribes in various parts
of Arabia, but doubtless the hellenistic formulations of their
teaching had little to commend it to other Arabs, whose
traditional culture was non-philosophical and close to that
of the Jews.

After Muhammad's death in 632 the state he had founded
developed rapidly into a large empire. It is completely
mistaken, however, to see this as an expansion of Islam by
the sword. For one thing, Christians, Jews and other
'peoples of the Book' were accepted as 'protected minorities'
within the Islamic state, and indeed at times were discour-
aged from becoming Muslims because this meant a loss of
taxes. Some modern Muslim writers claim that these con-
quering Muslim armies went, as it were, with the sword in
one hand and the Qur'ān in the other, but this is not borne

out by the historical records. The ordinary Arabs, and later the other peoples who took part in the wars of expansion, seem to have been chiefly interested in obtaining booty. What the military campaigns secured was the expansion of a political Islamic empire. It is also true, of course, that once non-Muslims had been accepted as 'protected minorities' within the empire, there were certain social pressures on them to become Muslims. Though relatively few Jews and Christians yielded to the pressures, in Iran the majority of the Zoroastrians did, because the Zoroastrian religion had lost much of its religious meaning and had become little more than a department of state.

Whatever their previous religion, the number of Muslims in the newly acquired provinces certainly increased, despite the fact that until 750 or later non-Arab Muslims had to become 'clients' of an Arab tribe. In the course of time this influx led to cultural problems. Islam originated in an Arab culture which was not dissimilar to Jewish culture in having little orientation to philosophy. By its expansion into Egypt, Syria, Iraq and Iran, Islam eventually came into contact with the modified hellenism of these regions. In Iraq there were colleges teaching Greek science, medicine and philosophy, and for a long time the 'Abbasid caliphs of Baghdad had a Christian as court physician. Converts with a previous hellenistic education may have played a part in introducing Greek ideas into Islamic theology, but we hear rather of born Muslims who realized that Greek forms of argument could help them in their disputes with other Muslims and with non-Muslims. The majority of these people belonged to the sect of the Mu'tazila, which flourished in the first half of the ninth century CE. In their enthusiasm for Greek ideas they adopted doctrines which most religious scholars regarded as heretical. About 900, however, the theologian al-Ash'ari, who had had a Mu'tazilite training, decided to use their methods to defend the doctrines of mainstream Islam. This led to the development of the discipline of Kalām or philosophical theology, which has continued ever since, and which became even more hellenized in about 1100 when another theologian, al-Ghazālī, introduced further aspects of Greek philosophy.

This hellenizing trend was vigorously opposed in the ninth century by Aḥmad ibn-Ḥanbal, who has given his name to the Hanbalite legal school; and in subsequent centuries his followers have maintained their rejection of the methods of Kalām. While keeping close to a literal interpretation of basic texts, they realized that the literal application to God of terms like hand and face was not possible; and, as mentioned in chapter 1, they held that such terms were to be understood amodally, that is, without asking how they were to be understood, whether literally or metaphorically. This line of thought has continued in Islam until the present day, as well as the more philosophical Kalām. Because Islam has no body corresponding to the Christian ecumenical councils, but operates rather on the basis of an informal consensus, these opposing trends of thought have managed to continue in existence side by side. In this way Islam may perhaps be said to have been more successful than Christianity in dealing with cultural differences.

Although Islam has no ecumenical councils, there is in each Islamic state what may be called a 'religious institution', namely, the powerful body of accredited jurists or ulema. In the past most Muslim rulers acknowledged the right of this body to formulate in detail the laws and rules of conduct based on the Shari'a or divinely given law, which itself is based on the Qur'ān and on the Sunna or practice of Muhammad. In the Ottoman empire until about 1850 this body controlled the formulation and administration of law, and all higher education, since jurisprudence was central to that, but after that date it lost much of its power. Something similar is true in other Islamic countries. Nevertheless in most countries the religious institution has used its influence to exclude from the consciousness of ordinary Muslims all that it considered contrary to basic mainstream Islam. This is probably the factor which has contributed most to the near-monolithic character of the culture which prevails today among the many diverse peoples of the Islamic world. One could, of course, ask whether they had dealt with the problem of cultural diversity or merely covered it over. There is something here worthy of further investigation.

In all these matters, including the growth of Islam to become the second largest religion in the world after Christianity, and to embrace about a fifth of the human race, I believe we should see something of the activity of God, especially since in the Biblical view he is active in all human history.

CHAPTER 6

The Religions in Today's World

It is now time to look at the problems which all the religions have to face in today's world, and which they will continue to face in tomorrow's world unless they find solutions.

Today's World and Its Problems

It is important to realize that today we are living in an age which is completely different in many respects from every previous age in world history. We now live in what has been described as a global village. This situation has been brought about by the development of science and technology. Travel and transport have been made easier and greatly speeded up. Jules Verne in 1873 imagined a journey 'Round the World in Eighty Days', and it required considerable ingenuity to accomplish the feat. Nowadays anyone who goes to a travel agency can book a flight to take them round the world in less than eighty hours. Statesmen now regularly fly half way round the world to have one or two days' talks with other statesmen. This, combined with the easier transport of goods, has meant that it is possible for millions of people to live together in vast conurbations. All this has come about through the invention and improvement of steam engines and steamships, motor vehicles and finally aeroplanes.

At the same time the invention of the telephone, radio

and television has greatly speeded up the communication of ideas. News, and what passes for news, flashes round the world in minutes. An event in one country may cause a riot on the other side of the world a few hours later. It has become difficult to keep anything completely hidden. Moreover, the media are beginning to have great power over the thinking and outlook on life of most of the citizens of a country. What the newspapers, radio and television present as interesting is eagerly seized upon by most people, and they unconsciously accept the values implicit in such presentations. In democratic countries the media are, of course, responding in part to what people want. Television in particular is concerned to achieve large audiences for its programmes. Yet the media may also in part be owned by big business, and this means that they encourage the values of consumerism. Where there is a strong autocratic ruler the media may be completely subservient, so that the mass of the people may be unaware that there is any way of under-standing current political and historical events other than the ruler's, since this alone is presented to them in the media.

Also implicit in the presentations of the media, but found too in serious books and publications, is what I call the Western intellectual outlook. This is the world-view which has developed from the thinking of the European Enlighten-ment in the eighteenth century. That movement maintained the ability of human reason to solve all problems, and was extremely critical of traditional organized Christianity. The more extreme views of the Enlightenment have few exponents nowadays, but there is a widespread secularism associated with the Western intellectual outlook. This out-look is assumed by the writers of scientific and other serious books, since it fully accepts the general scientific position. It is not always anti-religious, but tends to leave religion aside. Christian thinkers have been trying to come to terms with all this for over a century, and many have managed to reconcile the Western intellectual outlook with Christianity, at least to their own satisfaction; but there is as yet no official statement of Christian beliefs in accordance with this Western intellectual outlook.

With the formation of the global village this Western intellectual outlook has now spread to all parts of the world. All religions are having to come to terms with it, since many of their adherents think in this way on secular matters. Because this outlook, though secular, is not basically anti-religious, it should be possible for religions to accept most of it, but much deep and fundamental thinking is clearly required. The three Abrahamic religions have similar conceptions of God, and so their scholars ought to be able to help one another in the tasks before them.

Another distinctive feature of today's world as a result of advances in science and technology is the plentiful supply of the necessities of life and also of comforts and luxuries now available to human beings. This is particularly the case in the First World, but it is also increasingly true for sections of the population of the less wealthy countries. In the First World people have now come to expect a constantly rising standard of material living. What is called consumerism perhaps developed naturally when goods became plentiful, but it has also been encouraged by those with economic power, because they want to increase their profits by producing and selling more goods. New gadgets are constantly being invented which save a small amount of time, though it is doubtful whether they improve the quality of human life. What is clear, however, is that there is now immense economic power in the hands of a few individuals, such as the heads of multinational companies, and that these persons, even without breaking the rules currently accepted as governing business operations, can seriously impair the environment for the whole human race. They may also increase the relative poverty of many developing countries by paying unduly low wages for work done and the lowest possible rates for goods bought. The comfortable people in the First World, enjoying a high standard of living, should be deeply ashamed of the fact that this has in part been achieved for them by leaving millions of people starving to death in other parts of the world.

Again, since there has been a vast flood of labour-saving inventions, today's world in its richer parts is characterized by the fact that far fewer working hours are needed to keep everyone alive and comfortable. This has two important consequences. The first is that people have much more leisure time. In itself this might be a very good thing, if people knew how to use time creatively, but unfortunately many people have not had the opportunity to learn how to be creative. The experience of boredom has probably contributed to the increase in largely promiscuous sexual activity.

The other consequence is that there has been a great increase in unemployment in the First World and many other countries. Some First World leaders hope to solve the problem by increasing industrial development and so creating fresh jobs, but this would seem to imply increasing the amount of goods available in a situation where these are already plentiful, and where it is doubtful if additions would really enhance the quality of human life.

The New Position of the Religions

The fact that the world in which we now live differs from all previous ages affects the religions in two ways. They intermingle with one another to a greater extent than ever before, and they all have to face new problems.

In the description of our world in the previous section there were indications of the new problems which have to be faced. The products of Western science-based technology, such as cars and television sets, have spread all over the world, and adherents of all religions who can afford them want to have them, while the statesmen want Western armaments. It is virtually impossible, however, for a community to have these Western products without also becoming open to the whole secularist intellectual outlook of the West. For a long time the traditionalist Muslim religious scholars tried to prevent these Western ideas from contaminating the minds of Muslims, and something of that attitude still persists; but it seems clear to the outside observer that the battle has been lost. Some Islamic countries have now become enamoured of World Cup football. All the religions, including Christianity, have to face the problems created by the new situation. The two following sections will deal in more detail with the intellectual and practical problems, while the rest of the present section will consider further the relation of the religions to one another.

Something has already been said in chapter 5 about the fact that until two or three centuries ago the adherents of the great religions mixed little with one another. Each religion tended to be dominant in particular regions of the world and to determine the form of culture there. Even where adherents of different religions lived side by side they usually had no

contact at the purely religious level. Thus European mer-
chants on business visits to the Ottoman empire would rarely
discuss religion with Muslims there. Since about 1950,
however, countless Muslims, Hindus and others have come
to settle in Europe and North America, and some have
managed to fit in well with the local communities. In the
small town of Stornoway on the isle of Lewis in the west of
Scotland there is a flourishing group of Muslims who have
become partly Gaelic-speaking.[9] Where there are such close
connections religion is bound to be discussed at least
occasionally.

In the past the great religions regarded one another as
enemies. In the early centuries of the Christian era there
were bitter polemics between Jews and Christians, each
attacking the other and putting up defences against attacks
on themselves. Something similar has happened wherever
there has been a degree of contact between two religions.
Frequently, part of a religion's self-defence has been to form
a negative image of the other religion. When much of Spain
was under Muslim rule (from the eighth to the fifteenth
centuries CE) many Christians were in a difficult position,
because the Muslims were not only in political control but
were also culturally superior. With the backing of their
scholars the Christians came to adopt views about Islam
which placed it in a bad light; for example, that it was
sexually lax and that it spread by the sword, not by
convincing people of its truth. This enabled the Christians
to feel that in religion they were superior to the Muslims,
even though they were politically and culturally inferior.
Somewhat similarly, when in the seventh century CE Islam
spread into various provinces of the eastern Roman empire
and came into contact with Christians of a superior culture,

the Muslims formed a negative image of Christianity as a religion based on scriptures which were not genuine but had been corrupted and falsified. The negative images of other religions thus formed are often accompanied by an excessively favourable image of one's own religion, and this can make co-operation between religions difficult. It takes a considerable degree of humility to correct this inflated perception of one's own religion.

In all religions there are nowadays groups which have gone in the opposite direction. They claim to be returning to the true form of their religion as it was in the past, but they go on to assert the superiority of this form to all other forms of their own religion and of other religions. In Christianity there are extreme right-wing groups who firmly maintain that their way of expressing Christian belief is the only true one. In the United States, because of the growing political influence of this 'radical right' it has come to be felt as a threat to religious freedom, and an organization called the Interfaith Alliance has been formed by moderate Catholic, Protestant and Jewish leaders in order to oppose this threat. One Catholic leader said, 'As I see it, the radical right is creating divisiveness and narrowness on many complex religious and moral truths, rather than enlightenment and understanding.' A Jewish leader said, 'To equate human beings who are not like you, and with whom you disagree, to termites to be destroyed (as a radical Christian evangelist had done) is to use language frighteningly similar to that of the Nazis when they exterminated my brothers and sisters ... It is not just Jews who will suffer under the agenda being promoted by the religious right – it is anyone who may be different from the majority.'[10]

Christians should keep such facts in mind when they look

at their own and other religions, and realize that the extreme groups are mostly small minorities, and that there are many moderates who do not share their views. In Islam there are the so-called fundamentalists. In Judaism there are groups associated with extreme forms of political Zionism. Even Hinduism has some such groups. In all these groups political aims may be stronger than religious aims, and this tends to bring them into the limelight.[11] How their co-religionists are to deal with them is far from obvious. In the long term, however, as the central bodies in the religions successfully come to terms with the modern world, one would hope that these extreme groups would gradually die away. The rest of what I have to say applies mainly to these more central groups.

Despite the existence of extremists in the various religions, my personal view is that in the world of today the religions are no longer rivals or enemies, but should learn to see themselves as partners who have to deal with common problems. The obvious route for achieving such a partnership is summed up in the idea of dialogue. This covers many forms of conversation, from that among a few personal friends to those sponsored by the World Council of Churches and that in Tripoli, Libya, in 1976 sponsored by Colonel Gaddafi. Part of the purpose of dialogue is to enable members of one religion to learn from members of another what these find of value in their religion. In this way each should be able to correct the negative images they hold of the other religions and come to a more positive appreciation of their strengths, while at the same time attaining to a sounder appreciation of some aspects of their own faiths.

The importance of such appreciation of other religions

for one's personal growth to religious maturity is emphasized by Thomas Merton. He writes:

> The more I am able to affirm others, to say 'yes' to them in myself, by discovering them in myself and myself in them, the more real I am. I will be a better Catholic, not if I can *refute* every shade of Protestantism, but if I can affirm the truth in it and still go further. So too with the Muslims, the Hindus, the Buddhists, etc.[12]

He would see this as applying in the case of all the great religions, including Judaism. It is dubious, however, whether there would be much point in applying it to primitive religions or to phenomena such as the German-Christians of the Hitler period.

A precondition of true dialogue is that there should be no attempt to convert members of the other religion. Indeed the participants in formal religious dialogue should normally be persons well rooted in their own faith. When a deeper positive appreciation of the other religion's values is achieved, it will be seen that persons well grounded in it will be unlikely to gain anything from a change of religious allegiance, and might rather suffer loss if it meant a break with their present community. At the present time I either know personally, or know about, many Muslims who are doing excellent work for their fellow-Muslims and often also for other people, and it is impossible to see how a change of allegiance would make them better as individuals or enable them to do better work.

Because of such facts it is necessary in today's world to reconsider the ideas underlying much of the Christian missionary work of the last two hundred years, where the primary aim was to convert the 'heathen' and bring them into the Christian Church. Early history certainly shows examples where conversion was appropriate and led to good results. In the lifetime of Jesus and in the period after his death many Jews were excluded from experiencing the full satisfaction in life that their religion should have made possible; and in the Roman empire there were large numbers of people who were spiritually starved. To many in these groups Christianity brought new life. The earliest missionary spread of Islam occurred in similar circumstances. At the time of Muḥammad there was a spiritual vacuum in Arabia, and also among certain groups in the surrounding world, especially in Iran.

There were similarities and differences in the situation confronting the Christian missionary movement which began about 1800. While the conversion of the heathen to Christianity was in the forefront, there was also, at least in part, the idea of bringing spiritual life to those who lacked it. The movement, however, was also mixed up with the spread of European culture and with European colonialism. The missionaries had negative images of other religions, and they tended to assume that there was nothing of value in Islam and Hinduism, and certainly not in the African traditional religions. The measure of success which the missionaries achieved was chiefly in Africa and in disadvantaged Hindu groups, where they did bring a degree of new life; but they made few converts from Islam. Many of those who became Christians, of course, may have been attracted chiefly by the benefits of European culture.

In the closing years of the twentieth century there are again similarities and differences in the situation facing would-be missionaries of any religion. Non-Christians may now accept as much European culture as they want without becoming Christians. Secularism, however, has been weakening the influence of religion in many communities, so that all over the world there is a spiritual hunger which the religions ought to be able to relieve. The question is how this is to be brought about. In some places there are certainly marginal communities where conversion, that is, change of religious allegiance, is appropriate. Mostly, however, the spiritual hunger would be lessened if people could be brought to a fuller and better understanding of their own religion, and this should be the first priority. There may indeed be individual cases where special features make a change of religious allegiance the best way of meeting a person's deep spiritual needs; but such cases would be exceptional.

While change of religious allegiance should thus be given a secondary place, it is of great importance that each religion should present to adherents of other religions its understanding of the truth about the world. This will indeed occur in formal dialogue, but there are also other suitable occasions. As already noted, this helps to correct the existing negative images of other religions, while what is presented by others often leads to fresh insights into neglected aspects of one's own religion. There is much to be said for Thomas Merton's idea of affirming the truth in the other and then going further.

When the central groups of the various religions have reached some understanding of the truth in the other religions, and when they have come to realize the iconic or pictorial character of statements of religious belief, they should be able to see the other religions as partners and not rivals. All religions are concerned to give their adherents a conception of the world in which they have to live, of the values to be aimed at which make human life meaningful, and of the higher powers which have a degree of control over human life. The assertions of each religion must be taken as a whole, but, when this is done, I would hope that all would realize that their total presentations of ultimate truth are largely in agreement despite the differences in terminology. It is because of this that they are partners in the struggle against anti-religious forces in the world, such as secularism and materialism.

When Christians are presenting their understanding of ultimate truth to members of other religions, there should be considerable emphasis on the achievement of Jesus (as described in chapter 4). This presentation, however, should be in terms of his humanity and without the later theological interpretations. The other religions should then be allowed to understand it in their own terminology, and this could lead to interesting results. Christians, of course, claim that Jesus achieved something for humanity as a whole which no one else has achieved, and also think that nothing comparable has been achieved by a member of any other religion. If another religion claims that it has achieved something similar though in a different way, Christians should certainly look closely at the claim.

It is impossible to foresee in any detail what the outcome of such programmes might be. My hope is that all religions would come to see that Jesus had done something important, even if they did not fully accept the Christian understanding of his achievement. From this they might go forward to some formal acceptance of one another as partners. At the time of writing it seems unlikely that in the foreseeable future any religion will gain large numbers of converts from the others, and that means that they will have to manage to live side by side in harmony. Will there eventually be a single religion for the whole world? My feeling is that, while this is desirable, it should not be a monolithic religion, but one which allowed people from different cultural backgrounds to express ultimate truth in their own terms — something not unlike a comity of religions.

The Intellectual Problems Confronting the Religions

The basic intellectual problem confronting all the religions is that the secularist Western intellectual outlook has spread to every part of the world. It is being propagated by the media to such an extent that the most intelligent adherents of all the religions are exposed to it. They may even have imbibed much of this outlook without being aware of having done so. As was said above, it is not necessarily anti-religious, but it tends to squeeze religion out. Consequently all the religions now require to restate their basic truths in a form compatible with this outlook, or at least with most of it. There may be points in it which they think have to be denied completely.

The first problem to be considered is that raised for the Christian belief in God; but much of what is said will probably also be relevant to the Jewish and Islamic conceptions of God. As a result of intellectual movements in Europe from the Enlightenment or before, the conception of God seems to have been eroded or emasculated for most Christians. Their view of God is partly that of the deists; they think of God as the great First Cause who initiated the cosmic process and then left it largely to its own devices.

Christians may at times have an awareness of the presence of God or may have inner promptings which they believe are from God. But that is all. Apart from the few Christians who hold that God is active in their lives, God is mostly seen as very remote from everyday life. People have lost the Biblical conception of the God who is continuously creative in the world, and who is exercising a degree of control over the events of human history. These are aspects of belief in God which it is important to recover.

The fundamental question seems to be: Is this world in which we live and all the things in it the result of a 'fortuitous concourse of atoms', as has been suggested? When I look at the complexity of even a small creature like a fly, with a vast number of parts all contributing to enabling it to maintain its life and continue its species, I cannot believe that this has been brought about by pure chance. Somehow or other intelligent purpose has been involved in producing this result. The concourse of atoms has not been fortuitous, but has somehow been controlled. When one further considers how suitable the world is on the whole for human beings to lead pleasant and meaningful lives, it seems incredible that this could come about by chance. There must be some intelligent and benevolent purpose behind it.

This line of thought is reinforced when we think how wonderful human beings are. They have consciousness, but how can a complex collection of atoms have consciousness? Each has a mind and a memory. Even ordinary persons know several thousand words of their language, and remember thousands of facts about their past, the people they have met, the places where they have been, not to mention more general matters of geography, history and current events. Some people know several languages well. Very intelligent persons might conceivably know a million facts or more. Science tells us that this is accomplished by the atoms and molecules of our brains; but this does not explain the manner of its happening. It is in a sense miraculous, but the miracle is not God interfering with natural processes, but God working through and controlling natural processes.

Once life had appeared on earth there was a degree of intelligence and purpose in it which could have accounted for some of the phenomena; but it is far from obvious how even purposeful and intelligent vital forces could have produced the marvel of human life. It requires something like God. Then there is the question of how life developed from non-life, whether by a deep underlying movement towards greater complexity and greater consciousness, as Teilhard de Chardin thought, or in some other way.

For the Bible the appearance and evolution of human life on earth was not a fortuitous accident. It was implicit in the original act of creation. It was expressed pictorially and iconically by saying that God made men and women in his image. In terms of the current Western outlook we may think of creation as the initiation of the cosmic process, but this initiation was the work of a Being with something of a human aspect in him, namely, that of which human beings were the image; and the whole was directed from the beginning towards the realization of an ideal human community, which the Bible speaks of as the new Jerusalem. For the Bible, too, and also for the Qur'ān, creation is more than the initiation of the cosmic process – God creates each human being (e.g. Jeremiah 1:5; Sura 22:5).

In the chapter on the Old Testament it was emphasized that the writers understood all the main events of their history as having come about by the activity of God – the choice of Abraham, the Exodus from Egypt, the establishment of the kingdom by David, the sending of the great prophets, even the Exile and Restoration. They saw the non-Jew Cyrus being used as an instrument for God's purposes. The New Testament writers see the mission of John the Baptist and then that of Jesus as a continuation of the activity of God on behalf of his special people. Much of the activity of God in these events falls under two heads: calling or guiding an individual to a particular task; and strengthening him to achieve the task. Abraham was called on to leave his homeland; Moses was called on to return to Egypt and effect the deliverance of the Hebrew people from serfdom and genocide. David was strengthened to overcome his enemies in battle. God may also act in other ways, however. Perhaps, while strengthening David, he was also weakening his enemies.

In the Roman empire Christians were strengthened to maintain their faith against persecution, until in the fourth century Christianity became the religion of the empire. This development should be seen as having God's activity underlying and supporting it. The general expansion of Christianity in Europe should also be seen as coming about through God's supporting activity. It has been suggested above, however, that the expulsion of the oriental Christians (Copts, Jacobites, Nestorians, Armenians) from the Church was mistaken and contributed to the expansion of Islam, though Islam also is to be seen as being supported by divine activity.

A difficult question is whether we can discern the activity of God in recent and contemporary events. One can make suggestions, but one cannot always be sure that they are correct. Personally I feel that the change of policy in the

Soviet Union initiated by Mikhail Gorbachev can be seen as due to an inner prompting from God, even if he himself did not think of it in that way. I would also hold that, if the First World and other wealthy nations allow their economic policies to be dictated by greed, and fail to do something to reduce poverty in the developing world, they will suffer retribution in some form or another. We have to balance such suggestions, however, with the insistence of some of the prophets that God is preparing a better world for his people. While much of the suffering of the human race is due to the actions of other human beings, there are also natural disasters that we find inexplicable. Here we have to accept the message of the book of Job: these are indeed disasters, but they are not a reason for disbelieving in God.

From all these considerations we get the picture of God as a Being who is continually bringing into existence the many things in our world, and who exercises a degree of control over human history. Because of the limitations of our intellects we can have no precise conceptions of this Being. The words we use give us only a rough idea of what he is. Such conceptions as we have, however, are sufficiently true to provide a satisfactory basis for our daily living. If one likes to call this conception of God a theory, that is allowable; but then it must be insisted that this is a theory which has been a basis for living for millions of Jews, Christians and Muslims over many generations, and has proved satisfactory. Thus it is a theory that is justified by its fruits.

How is such a belief in God to be related to science? In the physical world science is most at home where it can find mathematical formulae. In the Biblical conception of God, however, there is nothing mathematical, and the intellectual ideas involved are imprecise. What I would say, however, is that if belief in God is regarded as an overriding theory, then within this theory, if scientists accept it, there is room for them to study all the physical and mathematical details of how the world came into being and other similar matters. If scientists decide that the universe began with a Big Bang, believers in God will accept that; and it is not too dissimilar from the Biblical account, although the latter is pictorial and iconic. Believers, however, could equally well accept some other account if scientists prefer that.

While belief in God is the most serious problem for the religions arising from the Western intellectual outlook, there are others. That outlook has a historical as well as a scientific side. It contributed to the development of the disciplines of historical and literary criticism. In previous chapters the problems these raised for Christians have been discussed. Though Muslims in general have been unwilling to make any use of literary criticism, it is unlikely that it will raise any serious problems for them, since the Qur'ān was never re-edited as Biblical books were. The chief concern of literary criticism would be with the dating of various passages and perhaps the question of whether there had been some revision. Islam is likely to have problems with historical criticism, however. Muslims often claim that the age of Muhammad and the rightly guided caliphs (to 661) was an ideal time; but this claim leaves aside many incidents that were far from ideal. Another point of conflict is the evaluation of the Umayyad caliphate (661–750), because the anti-Umayyad propaganda of the Roman period has been given almost official status; but many of the criticisms of the Umayyads are not borne out by contemporary documents.

Practical Problems Confronting the Religions

Before speaking in detail about particular practical problems which are now becoming urgent, it will be helpful to think about the ideal of human life in general. A picture of this is given in a sentence by Thomas Merton:

> A society built on Christian principles is one in which every man has the right and opportunity to live in peace, to support himself by meaningful, decent and productive work, work in which he has a considerable share of responsibility, work which is his contribution to the balance and order of a society in which a reasonable happiness is not impossible. [13]

Leaders in other religions would probably agree that they too are aiming to bring about a society something like this. Such a society as an ideal is indeed implicit in the nature of human life. Human beings do not make themselves. They are not even made by their parents; though the parents have to make decisions, they do no more than hand on the power of life they themselves received. Because of the character of this life they have been given, people have various basic urges. One is to maintain their own individual lives, and another is to maintain the life of the species by producing children. They cannot properly satisfy these urges without some sort of community, and it is desirable that there should be a large measure of harmony within this community – something which requires basic rules such as respect for life, property and marriage. There is also, however, a deep urge to achieve a meaningful life, and this urge is largely satisfied when a person has work to do which contributes in some way or other to maintaining and possibly improving the life of the community. This is the sort of thinking behind what Thomas Merton said about work.

A more theological Christian statement of all this would be to say that people are set in this world by God to do his will. This will is primarily that each individual should share in work for maintaining the human community and leading it to ever higher attainments. Other religions would probably say something similar, though in their own terminology. The immediate question is whether they can co-operate in any way in order to further such aims in this world of today, in which many forces are moving in an opposite direction.

A quotation from Thomas Merton may again help:

The central problem of the modern world is the complete emancipation and autonomy of the technological mind at a time when unlimited possibilities lie open to it and all the resources seem to be at hand. Indeed, the mere fact of questioning this emancipation, this autonomy, is the number-one blasphemy, the unforgivable sin in the eyes of the modern man, whose faith begins with this: science can do everything, science must be permitted to do everything it likes, science is infallible and impeccable, all that is done by science is right. No matter how monstrous, no matter how criminal an act may be, if it is justified by science it is unassailable.

The consequence of this is that technology and science are now responsible to no power and submit to no control other than their own. Needless to say, the demands of ethics no longer have any meaning if they come in contact with these autonomous powers. Technology has its own ethic of expediency and efficiency. What *can* be done efficiently *must* be done in the most efficient way – even if what is done happens, for example, to be genocide or the devastation of a country by total war.[14]

A small facet of this matter has been attracting attention recently, namely, the discovery or invention of several new artificial methods of producing human babies. Some sections of public opinion are alarmed at the new possibilities, and are demanding that the ethical implications should be carefully scrutinized. What is possible is not always desirable. The central question is whether children produced in such ways would feel deprived or otherwise inferior.

What Thomas Merton says about science and technology has, of course, to be linked with the growth of immense economic power in multinational corporations and elsewhere. Those who wield this power are chiefly concerned with profits. Though they may not be doing anything contrary to contemporary business ethics, they may still be damaging the general quality of human life. They encourage consumerism in the countries of the First World and among the wealthier sections of the population in other countries. They keep inventing and advertising gadgets and luxuries in order to persuade people to buy them and so increase the profits of the manufacturers and retailers; but it is not seriously asked whether these are enhancing the quality of human life. The media are often under the control of the great economic powers, and encourage the consumerist attitude to life, while at the same time making a profit from their advertising.

The sort of question that might be asked here is: Is it necessary or desirable for you to have an electric toothbrush? Does the saving of time and energy really improve your life? Then one can go on to bigger questions: Is it necessary or desirable that so many individuals should have their own cars? Would it not be better to have more efficient systems of public transport? One of the results of the advances in science and technology is that far fewer working hours are now required to produce the basic necessities of human life, at least in the First World. So why reduce them further? As Thomas Merton said, it is important that every human being should have work to do which he or she feels is contributing to the welfare of the community. Many of the appliances recently invented, however, do not really improve human life, so is the work involved in manufacturing them contributing to the welfare of the community? And is the labour-saving aspect not worsening the problem of unemployment? Is it always good to replace people by machines?

Those with great economic power have often shown scant regard for the natural environment. They have used up scarce resources of unrenewable materials like iron. They have destroyed vast areas of equatorial forest containing valuable natural resources, and for relatively limited ends; and such forests cannot be renewed quickly, if at all. There are also many resulting forms of pollution.

It is obvious that the great economic power wielded today by some individuals cannot be controlled by a single state, however powerful. There has to be international control. This means a redesigning and strengthening of the United Nations or the finding of a replacement for it. At present many countries other than those of the First World tend to regard the United Nations as an instrument of American, or at least First World, policy. This is a point at which leaders of the world religions might be able to co-operate in helping to work out the principles on which an effective and impartial international body might be established.

A stronger United Nations or a replacement should be able to ensure that scarce natural resources are not wantonly destroyed merely to increase profits. It is also desirable that it should place severe restrictions on the Western arms industry, which has been making large profits by selling powerful weapons to dictatorial rulers and governments in the developing world and so making it possible for them to exert cruel forms of oppression over their own people. One would also expect this new United Nations to do what it could to bring about a fairer distribution of the necessities of life between the wealthy First World countries and the rest of the world. This problem, however, is mainly one for the wealthy countries themselves, who should be brought to see that it is in their own long-term interest to be satisfied with a slightly lower standard of living, while striving to promote greater equality in standards of living throughout the world. Without a measure of equality there will almost certainly be an explosive reaction of some sort.

Apart from the reform of the United Nations there are other problems where the religions might be able to work together, or at least along parallel lines. One is the growth of consumerism – really another word for greed – wherever there is wealth. Where people have the possibility of a higher standard of material living, there is a strong tendency for them to work for this, and this tendency is fanned by the advertisements of the economic giants. All the religions believe that there are more important things in human life than a high material standard of living; and of their adherents many accept this view, while a few form movements to try to correct present trends. In many ways consumerism is encouraged by the media, especially television, and the religions need to find ways of counteracting the influence of the media. This is not easy, of course, because the media need a degree of freedom to examine and report informatively and insightfully on government and society in general. Nevertheless, movements of resurgence in the religions have a part to play in maintaining a critical stance towards the uglier and less valuable aspects of our society, such as consumerism; and this may in turn influence the position of the media.

Finally there are the problems created by unemployment. It was suggested above that it is wrong to assume that saving labour is always a good thing. It is easy for companies to decide to install new labour-saving machines and then to dismiss staff, because this will slightly increase profits; but the companies may then face increased taxes in order to support the unemployed. Clearly it is important to look at all aspects of what is involved in 'progress'.

The problem of unemployment is a serious and difficult one. It is particularly serious in light of the point made by Thomas Merton that each human being should feel he or she has a task to perform which is contributing in one way or another to the welfare of the community. Increased unemployment, however produced, leads to increased leisure, and this can lead to boredom unless satisfactory ways are found of filling it. Football matches, musical events, the theatre and the cinema are ways of providing amusement, and those who are best at amusing the public make huge sums of money. Many ways of filling one's leisure, however, do not enhance the quality of human life. A small amount of television is good, but to spend six hours a day or more before the box is impairing the quality of one's life as a human being because of the passivity involved. In this matter the religions ought to be able to help. Each could encourage its adherents to spend more time in worship, prayer, meditation and other religious exercises, especially where there is a communal aspect.

Time devoted to religion in any way reduces the pressure from the secularism of the media. People could also be encouraged to join with others in various activities, especially those where there is an element of creativity. There is nearly always scope, too, for voluntary and informal social work, since most communities contain individuals who are suffering from various disabilities and misfortunes, temporarily or permanently. Such work is indeed already being done by some of the renewal groups which have appeared in the great religions in the last couple of decades. It is up to the leadership in the religions to develop such activities.

In this examination of practical problems there have been some, notably the reform of the United Nations, where it is desirable that the religions should formally co-operate. In other matters each may have to deal primarily with its own adherents as best it can. If, however, the religions realize that they are partners and not rivals, the sphere for co-operation should gradually increase, resulting in an improvement in the spiritual as well as material well-being of the many millions of people alive in the world today.

Notes

1. W.M. Watt, *Islam and Christianity Today* (London: Routledge, 1983), p. 119.
2. Harmondsworth: Penguin Books, 1971.
3. *The Tablet*, 8 January 1994, p. 9.
4. Especially in *Truth in the Religions* (Edinburgh University Press, 1963), pp. 126–8.
5. *Conjectures of a Guilty Bystander* (New York: Image Books, 1968), p. 33.
6. Ibid.
7. I now consider that my use of 'symbolic' in *Islam and Christianity Today* is confusing and should be replaced by 'iconic'.
8. *Studia Missionalia* (Rome), xlii (1993), pp. 245–55.
9. Akbar Ahmed, *From Samarkand to Stornoway: Living Islam,* (London: BBC Books, 1993).
10. *The Tablet*, 23 July 1994, p. 934.
11. Further details in Gilles Kepel, *The Revenge of God: The Resurgence of Islam, Christianity and Judaism in the Modern World* (Oxford, Polity Press, 1994).
12. *Conjectures*, p. 144.
13. Ibid., p. 94.
14. Ibid., p. 75.